D0060740

Faculty Towers

PERSONAL TAKES

An occasional series of short books in which noted critics write about the persistent hold particular writers, artists, or cultural phenomena have had on their imaginations.

Faculty Towers

The Academic Novel and Its Discontents

ELAINE SHOWALTER

PENN

UNIVERSITY OF PENNSYLVANIA PRESS

PHILADELPHIA

Copyright © 2005 Elaine Showalter
All rights reserved
Printed in the United States of America on acid-free paper

10 9 8 7 6 5 4 3 2 1

Published by
University of Pennsylvania Press
Philadelphia, Pennsylvania 19104-4011

Library of Congress Cataloging-in-Publication Data

Showalter, Elaine.
Faculty towers : the academic novel and its discontents / Elaine Showalter.
p. cm. — (Personal takes)
Includes bibliographical references (p.) and index.
ISBN 0-8122-3850-8 (cloth : alk. paper)
1. College stories, English—History and criticism. 2. College stories,
American—History and criticism. 3. English-speaking countries—
Intellectual life. 4. Teacher-student relationships in literature.
5. Universities and colleges in literature. 6. Education, Higher, in literature.
7. College teachers in literature. 8. College students in literature.
I. Title. II. Series.

PR830.U5S36 2005
823.009′3557—dc22
2004054977

Contents

Introduction: What I Read and What I Read For   1

chapter 1
  The Fifties: Ivory Towers   14

chapter 2
  The Sixties: Tribal Towers   34

chapter 3
  The Seventies: Glass Towers   49

chapter 4
  The Eighties: Feminist Towers   68

chapter 5
  The Nineties: Tenured Towers   87

chapter 6
  Into the Twenty-First Century: Tragic Towers   100

Conclusion   118

Notes   125

Bibliography of Academic Novels   133

Index   137

Acknowledgments   143

What I Read and
What I Read For

WHY IS THE ACADEMIC NOVEL my favorite literary genre? Maybe it's just narcissistic pleasure. One theory about the rise of the novel argues that it developed because readers like to read about their own world, and indeed about themselves. And yes, I am a professor of English literature, and yes, I have been a character in academic fiction at least twice, once a voluptuous, promiscuous, drug-addicted bohemian, once a prudish, dumpy, judgmental frump. I hope I am not too easily identified in either of these guises, and I'm not about to disclose the novels here, although I can tell you that I preferred being cast as the luscious Concord grape to my role as the withered prune.

Long before I was a professor, however, I was addicted to reading academic novels, whose popularity coincided with my own adolescence. The genre has arisen and flourished only since about 1950, when American universities were growing rapidly, first to absorb the returning veterans, and then to take in a larger and larger percentage of the baby-booming population. The nature of higher education in America and Britain had a lot to do with it too. Most of our universities act in loco parentis for students, creating a complete society on the campus, with housing, meals, medical care, and social life all provided communally and institutionally. They actively foster close personal relations between students and faculty. Moreover, the curriculum usually includes a program in creative writing; as a result, most faculties include a few professional writers who can observe the tribal rites of their colleagues from an insider's perspective.

Of course, students have long been important characters in fiction;

coming-of-age narratives and *Bildungsromane* have been numerous from early days. To me, however, the most interesting academic novels are about the faculty, the lifers—what one critic has called *Professorromane.*[1] I found these stories entertaining, inspiring, and instructive. In the 1960s, as a first-generation college graduate, I took an immigrant's passionate ethnographic interest in their details of academic manners. They filled a novice's need to fit into a culture, and I found answers, of a sort, to many of my questions and even to questions I hadn't formed. And decade by decade, as I became a professor myself and experienced the realities and diversities of colleges and universities, I measured the gap between what I lived and what I read. In an era before there were handbooks, self-help guides, or advice columns for graduate students and junior faculty in the *Chronicle of Higher Education,* novels taught me how a proper professor should speak, behave, dress, think, write, love, succeed, or fail. Now that I have retired, I read them less personally, but with more affection and empathy.

The academic novel is by now a small but recognizable subgenre of contemporary fiction and has a small body of criticism devoted to it. Most critics hold that it is basically satirical. According to Sanford Pinsker, in "Who Cares If Roger Ackroyd Gets Tenure?" "the general form is as old as Aristophanes' *The Clouds.* There, Socrates was held up to ridicule as a man riding through the heavens in a basket; and the label of dreamy impracticality stuck not only to him, but also to all the befuddled academic types who have followed."[2] Many academic novels are wildly funny, and lines from them have sustained me in hard times, from Lucky Jim's description of his ghastly little spider hole of a thesis as "this strangely-neglected topic" to the jokes in James Hynes's *The Lecturer's Tale.*

Yet strangely enough, what appeals to me most in academic fiction is its seriousness, even sadness. Perhaps we professors turn to satire because academic life has so much pain, so many lives wasted or destroyed. On the spelling corrector on my computer, when I click on English, the alternative that comes up is Anguish. Like the suburbs, the campus can be the site of pastoral, or the fantasy of pastoral—the refuge, the ivory tower. But also like the suburbs, it is the site of those perennials of the literary imagination John Updike names as "discontent, conflict, waste, sorrow, fear."[3]

Perhaps it's the ultimate narcissism for an English professor to write literary criticism about novels by English professors about English professors, but my favorite academic novels are about English departments nonetheless. Ian Carter says that academic novels are all predictable and indeed are mind-bogglingly repetitive: "I would pick up a novel newly discovered in a library stack or decayed secondhand bookshop," he writes. "It could belong to one of many genres; comedy of manners, thriller, whodunit, romance. After a couple of pages I would discover the awful truth. *I had read it before.* After a couple of years, I had read them all before."[4] But Carter is a sociologist, who embarked on his reading of academic fiction out of annoyance with Malcolm Bradbury's portrayal of sociologists in *The History Man.* For English professors, this repetitiveness also means that the novels operate on a set of conventions, themes, tropes, and values. Having read all the novels before gives us some distance on their narrative strategies and turns easy identification into something more intellectual.

Like other closed societies, the campus can function as a microcosm, according to Jay Parini, "a place where humanity plays out its obsessions and discovers what makes life bearable."[5] Steven Connor elaborates: "The university is a closed world, with its own norms and values, which is thick with the possibilities of intrigue. Indeed, the very restriction of elements in the academic world, with the stock characters, with their cosily familiar routines of evasion and abstraction and their conspicuous, if always insecure, hierarchical structures, and the well-established situations and plot-lines, seem to generate a sense of permutative abundance." Connor sees two basic plots in academic fiction: "The one concerns the disruption of a closed world, and the gradual return of order and regularity to it, while the other concerns the passage through this closed world of a character who must in the end be allowed to escape its gravitational pull."[6]

Janice Rossen thinks that the university novel is mainly about power, inclusion, and exclusion. "Like their counterparts in any other profession, academics delight in reinforcing this view of themselves as comprising circles which are closed to the uninitiated. They also tend to compete with each other within that realm for positions of power. Academic fiction almost always takes this competitiveness as part of its basis." Novels pull together "several disparate but related threads: the influence of the power structure within academe and in relation to the world outside, the constant dialectic between compet-itiveness and idealism—or, scholarship as a means to an end or as an end in itself—and the implications for the creative process of the novel-ist's choice of such a potentially limiting and problematic subject." And overall, "the more conflicting cross-currents a novelist is able to incorporate and contrast in a given work, the better the novel."[7]

Those formulas seem rather cut-and-dried to me. The best aca-demic novels experiment and play with the genre of fiction itself, comment on contemporary issues, satirize professorial stereotypes and educational trends, and convey the pain of intellectuals called upon to measure themselves against each other and against their in-ternalized expectations of brilliance. Sanford Pinsker, who is Ameri-can, thinks all English professors are frustrated novelists, attracted to fiction as a neat payback and a fast buck: "Which self-respecting lit professor hasn't thought—either out loud or in private—about knocking off a tale of the assorted troubles at his or her version of Eyesore U? After all, the formula seems simple enough: plant a sen-sitive young professor in a garden of academic vipers, add a fetching student here and a soused administrator there, and *voila*, yet another novel about higher education on the ropes."[8] But Steven Connor, who is British, writes with more circumspection that the real attrac-tion of the *Professorroman* to readers and writers is its double audi-ence of insiders and outsiders: "The fact that most campus novels tend to be about English teachers or students . . . is of course not very surprising even given the hostility to traffic or fraternization between the critical and creative realms characteristic of the teaching of English literature since the War. What is less often remarked is what this implies about the addressivity of such novels, which is to say their sense of their readership and the different attitudes to it that they may have."[9]

I'm not exactly sure what Connor means by addressivity. Certainly British academic novelists have gone further than Americans in experimenting with double narratives and clever literary allusions. But I suppose one less exalted implication of the "addressivity" of the English-professor novel could be the insider's gossipy pleasure in rec-ognizing portraits, usually unflattering, of colleagues and friends. I think I may recognize a few in the pages of recent books I have enjoyed, but who among us can be sure we are immune from such treatment? Are we smiling at the gallery of fruits, not noticing that we ourselves are the desiccated prune or the overripe grape?

Moreover, because we professors now live in the age of celebrity, publicity, and fame, being a character in a satiric academic novel, even a nasty one, may be a kind of distinction. Stanley Fish likes being identified with David Lodge's Morris Zapp; Laurie Taylor didn't mind being falsely thought to be the original History Man; and when Sandra Gilbert and Susan Gubar wrote a parody of the academic world called *Masterpiece Theater*, more people were offended because they were excluded than because they were mocked.

PRECURSORS

I suppose one of the reasons I like academic novels is their similiarity to Victorian ones, which I taught for many years. The academic novel proper doesn't start until the 1950s, but there are nineteenth-century precursors. Anthony Trollope's comic masterpiece *Barchester Towers* (1857) is the great ur-narrative of academic politics, even if it is about the bickering of provincial Anglican clergy over preferment and evangelical reform. Trollope's wrangling, rivalrous Victorian clerics remind me of contemporary academics, with assistant professors, deans, and provosts standing in for curates, deacons, and bishops; and many authors of academic fiction, from C. P. Snow on, have been Trollope scholars. If I ever write an academic novel myself, it will be called "Barchester University." The title of this book, *Faculty Towers*, is an amalgam of Barchester and the classic British TV sitcom of the dysfunctional and manic provincial hotel, Fawlty Towers, and its irascible manager, Basil Fawlty.

The supreme academic fiction remains *Middlemarch* (1872), and Eliot's Mr. Casaubon is the most haunting spectre of the academic as grim pedagogue, the scholar as the spirit of all that is sterile, cold, and dark. Casaubon has no small talk, but only a large, sad, musty talk of dead things. "I live too much with the dead," he says of himself. His pleasures are of "the severer kind"; his house, Lowick, has "an air of autumnal decline"; his smile is like "pale wintry sunshine"; he looks like "a death's head skinned over for the occasion." And yet Eliot has sympathy for "the despair which sometimes threatened him while toiling in the morass of authorship without seeming nearer to the goal." Casaubon uses all his meager energy in sustaining his self-esteem, in defending himself against the realization that his life's work of synthesis and theory, which Eliot in a stroke of prophetic insight titles the "Key to All Mythologies," is a hollow sham and that his "hard intellectual labours" have led only to "a melancholy absence of passion in his efforts at achievement, and a passionate resistance to the confession that he had achieved nothing."

"Achieved nothing": it's every scholar's most feared epitaph. When I entered the academic profession, in the early years of the women's liberation movement in the 1960s and 1970s, feminist academics read *Middlemarch* as a book about female ardour and longing for the epic life and then announced themselves disillusioned by Eliot's compromises of her heroine Dorothea's ambition. "As I have moved away from what I now believe was an adolescent fantasy concerning the contents and implications of *Middlemarch* to what I hope is a more true understanding of the text's attitudes toward woman," wrote Lee Edwards in 1972, "I see that it can no longer be one of the books of my life."[10] On the contrary, with every year that has passed since I got my Ph.D., *Middlemarch* has become more the canonical book of my academic life, the most eloquent of academic tragedies.

Another novel along the same lines, one that must have been influenced by Eliot, is Willa Cather's *The Professor's House* (1925). Cather too writes about the midlife crisis of a male academic, Godfrey St. Peter, burned-out although he is only fifty-two. Unlike Casaubon, St. Peter is a historian whose lifework, an eight-volume study of the *Spanish Adventurers in North America*, has won him acclaim, even the Oxford prize for history. But the meaning seems to have gone out of his life and his teaching; at the novel's conclusion, he is resigning himself to spending the remains of his days without delight: "Theoretically he knew that life is possible, may even be pleasant, without joy, without passionate griefs. But it had never occurred to him that he might have to live like that."[11]

Pretty dire introductions to the life of the mind, or at least the male life of the mind as seen by women novelists—the sacrifice of love to intellectual labor, the shriveling of unused emotions, the steady encroachment of a tumorous vanity. Its antitheses are not in great novels like these, but in popular fiction. Luckily I also read Dorothy L. Sayers's *Gaudy Night* (1936), set in Shrewsbury, a version of her own Oxford college, Somerville, revisited by her fictional detective Harriet Vane. Here, although there is vanity, greed, hypocrisy, and even murder in the female community of the college, the female dons are absorbed by their work and still alive to more worldly pleasures, including gossip, fashion, food, and drink. To be sure, the first one of them we hear is "a grizzled woman don crossing the turf with vague eyes, her thoughts riveted upon aspects of sixteenth-century philosophy, her sleeves floating" like some academic angel. But most of the women dons are brisk and open-minded in their interests. "We're not nearly such dried-up mummies as you think," the bright-eyed dean tells Harriet, echoing a description of Casaubon in *Middlemarch*: "He is no better than a mummy!" However sexless, arid, and withered the male academic may be, Sayers proves that the female academic does not have to copy him.

When English professors write novels, they tend to write about what they know best: other people's books. Even in some of the most celebrated and familiar academic satires, rewriting literary conventions is as important as mocking campus attitudes. Many of the best and most successful academic novels of the past fifty years have been rewritings of Victorian novels. In *Nice Work*, David Lodge rewrote the genre of the English industrial novel, particularly Elizabeth Gaskell's *North and South*, to describe the tensions between the modern university and the world of business. Gail Godwin based her academic novel *The Odd Woman* on Gissing's masterpiece about Victorian feminism, *The Odd Women*. Joanne Dobson's wonderful series about feminist professor Karen Pelletier is based on the nineteenth-century American women's novels Dobson has written about as a scholar. James Hynes's *Publish and Perish* rewrites and updates the Victorian horror tale, and A. S. Byatt's *Possession* creates its own archive of Victorian poetry.

ACADEMIC TIME

Novels about professors are set in academic time, which is organized and compartmentalized according to various grids and calendars, vacations and rituals. Some of the characters have names that allude to that system, such as Annie Callendar in *The History Man*. Traditionally, academics have been envied for their control of their time.

"Of all professional people," Hazard Adams (not a fictional character) has observed, "the scholar in a major university has probably the greatest degree of personal freedom to organize his day, month, and year."[12]

But as the costs of higher education rise, the scholar's use of time has come under increased external scrutiny and skepticism. Only two courses a semester? The summer off? What the hell do you people do? One of the classic genres of faculty prose is the account of a typical day in the life of a professor, usually published in the campus newspaper or alumni magazine and designed to impress deans, parents, and legislators with the single-minded diligence, seriousness, devotion to students, and sheer love of learning of the professor in question. These don's diaries are often infuriating to colleagues, who view them as highly competitive, inflated, self-important, and fictional. I remember a particularly notorious one in which the professor claimed to rise at 5:30 to prepare for his undergraduate seminar and continue nonstop intellectual, pedagogical, and administrative labors through a long day punctuated only by wholesome snacks, personal intervals to answer vast amounts of international e-mail, a recreational break to study Latin, and a meal out at a fine restaurant with wife and son and visiting dignitary. Female faculty sputtered over it for days.

But professorial time does seem both overloaded day to day and painfully drawn out and Beckettish year to year. On the microlevel, it can be divided into lectures, office hours, and department meetings. As John Kenneth Galbraith writes, "lectures are our most flexible art form. Any idea, however slight, can be expanded to fill fifty-five minutes; any idea, however great, can also be condensed to that time."[13] The achievements and disappointments of a career must be similarly expressed in the form of the C.V., which leaves out all the personal vicissitudes of a real life and a real year and which is also a flexible genre that can expand by listing talks to the local PTA. The C.V., updated annually for salary review, is an academic's diary or life record. "Sometimes I think that without a c.v. I could never reconstruct my life," writes Nancy Miller. "Having spent almost my entire life in school—first as a student, then as a teacher—I sometimes fear that my autobiography *is* my curriculum vitae."[14]

On the macrolevel, there is the sabbatical and the division of academic life into seven-year chunks. Carol Shields and Alison Lurie are among those who have written about the sabbatical in novels, where it is usually a time of transformation and epiphany. But there is also the pressure of the seven-year apprenticeship of junior faculty, customarily described in the metaphor of the ticking tenure clock, but more of a great Poe-like pendulum. The confrontations of tenure competition haven't really received their psychological due in academic fiction, although being turned down for tenure is one of the most stressful and traumatic events of a professional life. This is so not only for the individual but for the group, the department, or the college. For unlike the corporate world, the academy does not sever connections with its terminated faculty immediately. Assistant professors who are denied tenure don't clean out their desks and go home to stick pins in wax models of their colleagues.

What is peculiarly painful about the tenure process is its duration, its *longue durée*. The "terminated" assistant professor must linger for a year, or maybe two, continuing to carry out his duties, looking for another job, among senior colleagues who may have voted against him. Because of the confidentiality of the process, the candidate doesn't know for sure how the vote went, but there will be plenty of rumors and gossip. Meanwhile he has to be polite, to wear an elaborate social mask until he can leave; but so will most of his colleagues, who are struggling with their own survivors' guilt, bad faith, hypocrisy, pity, or just the wish not to be confronted with human suffering.

But the most common temporal metaphor for academic life is that of the four seasons. According to Hazard Adams, "the solar cycle of academic life balances the linear progression of the academic career." He sees the academic year divided into three parts, like Northrop Frye's literary archetypes: "The fall quarter, or hope; the winter quarter, or endurance; and the spring quarter, or anticipation."[15] Of course, some universities have semester systems, and many have summer sessions and summer programs like the School of Criticism and Theory, adding a fourth quarter (festival?) to the solar year.

In *The Department* (1968), Gerald Warner Brace gives a hauntingly medieval twist of fate to the image:

We go on doing the same things, going through the same yearly cycle; I think of it always as a great ferris wheel, beginning its upward turn in September, and all of us in the one bucket, as it were, mounting and turning over the crest and falling toward the summer with the same inexorable pace as the revolving seasons. I even think of the week as a small wheel, climbing from the low point of Monday upward and then over into Friday and down through the week's end. Routines go on like fate. The oddities and interruptions, the personals deaths and disasters, are all irrelevant. Perhaps all human worlds revolve in cycles, like the cosmic spheres, but I think the academic world is more obviously geared that way than any other. It is half aware of its old, old machinery that dates back to some remote medieval age in Bologna or Oxford, it goes through familiar rituals without quite knowing why or wherefore, it sustains visions of ideal detachment, it believes that wisdom is without date or current alteration. Many of us come to depend wholly on the academic cycles, great and small, to revolve us safely from boyhood to death.[16]

For academics, autumn is the beginning. "Despite the challenges of teaching," writes Jay Parini, "it's hard not to like a job where you can start over every September, shredding the previous year's failures and tossing them out the window like so much confetti." Time seems to stand still: "The slate is theoretically wiped clean in September, and one is given a fresh packet of chalk. The clock is rewound, and the faces before one never seem to age (except in faculty meetings, where only those who never question anything are without deep lines in their foreheads)." Yet the renewal of fall seems unnatural: "The rhythm of education runs counter to natural grieving. According to the academic calendar, fall means starting over, springing into life after the torpid drowse of summer. There is, indeed, a vague sense of dislocation as classes begin and as the first faculty meetings occur against a backdrop of whirling leaves and days that seem woefully tinged at dusk."[17]

Novelists play on the ironic ambiguities of that autumnal start. Malcolm Bradbury begins *The History Man* with a report on the season:

Now it is the autumn again; the people are all coming back. The recess of summer is over, when holidays are taken, newspapers shrink, history itself seems momentarily to falter and stop. But the papers are thickening and filling again; things seem to be happening; back from Corfu and Sète, Positano and Leningrad, the people are parking their cars and campers in their drives and opening their diaries, and calling up other people on the telephone. . . . The new autumn colors are in the boutiques; there is now on the market a fresh intra-uterine device, reckoned to be ninety-nine per cent safe. Everywhere there are new developments, new indignities; the intelligent people survey the autumn world, and liberal and radical hackles rise, and fresh faces are about, and the shine shines fitfully, and the telephones ring.[18]

Winter in the university is different from winter elsewhere. Although it is a time of darkness, it also a time of respite and escape. In *The History Man*: "and now it is the winter again; the people, having come back, are going away again. The autumn, in which the passions rise, the tensions mount, the strikes accumulate, the newspapers fill with disaster, is over. Christmas is coming; the goose is getting fat, and the papers getting thin; things are stopping happening. In the drives, the cars are being packed, and the people are ready, in relief to be off, to Positano or the Public Record Office, Moscow or mother, for the lapse of the festive season."[19] In a certain kind of British, or Anglophile, academic novel, such as Snow's *The Masters*, Byatt's *Possession*, or Donna Tartt's *The Secret History*, winter is a time of heightened privacy, inwardness, even eroticism. *The Masters* begins with a sensuous celebration of the pleasures of winter and solitary study (perhaps a novelist named Snow felt a natural affinity for the season):

> The snow had only just stopped, and in the court below my rooms all sounds were dulled. . . . It was scorchingly hot in front of the fire, and warm, cosy, shielded, in the zone of the two armchairs and the sofa which formed an island of comfort round the fireplace. Outside that zone, as one went towards the walls of the lofty medieval room, the draughts were bitter . . . so that, on a night like this, one came to treat most of the room as the open air, and hurried back to the cosy island in front of the fireplace, the pool of light from the reading lamp on the mantelpiece, the radiance which was more pleasant because of the cold air which one has just escaped.[20]

It's an apt metaphor for the scholar's life.

But in spring, especially in American universities, this cosy exile is invaded, and there is trouble brewing for the faculty from the administration and the students. The administration is plotting: "April is the month of heightened paranoia for academics," writes Richard Russo, "not that their normal paranoia is insufficient to ruin a perfectly fine day in any season. But April is always the worst. Whatever dirt will be done to us is always planned in April, then executed over the summer, when we are dispersed."[21]

The students are protesting, as Mary McCarthy explains: "The whole campus was, as usual, unsettled by the vernal influence and the prospect of Easter vacation: hitherto well-satisfied students came before the department wanting to change their major or their tutor and were dissuaded with the greatest difficulty: room-mates broke up; love affairs were blighted; girls wept in the wash-room; Miss Rejnev's Russian literature class sent her a petition that they had had enough of Dostoievsky."[22]

The transition from spring to summer brings commencement exercises and class reunions; their juxtaposition must make the meanest professorial intellect reflect on time and mortality. At Princeton, the highlight of annual class reunions, which take place in early summer, just before graduation, is called the P-rade. Reunion classes march through the campus, dressed in orange and black blazers of different patterns, or orange and black costumes suggesting the cultural or political themes of their graduation year—spacemen, soldiers, Arabs, hippies. They march in order of age, from the oldest to the youngest; at the head of the procession are the oldest living members of the class of whatever, riding in electric cars, gallantly waving to the cheering spectators. The procession is a hallowed literary metaphor, but this one is especially resonant, like the mummers on the horizon of Bergman's *The Seventh Seal*. Behind the cheering alumni and the antique autos, I always imagine, should be death's winged chariot, with a tall figure in an orange and black hooded robe carrying a scythe.

Because of the importance of academic time, I have organized this book chronologically by decades. Chronology is not a perfect organizational instrument for fiction, of course. Academic novels are rarely in synch with their decade of publication; most reflect the preceding decade's issues, crises, and changes. Some themes are so recurrent that I have treated them out of chronological order. But in general, reading academic novels from 1950 to the present gives a good overview of the way the academy and its scribes have moved from hope to endurance to anticipation to cynicism and around to hope again.

Faculty Towers is not intended to be a comprehensive history of the Anglo-American academic novel over the past fifty years. It's a personal take, and my selection reflects my preoccupations, particularly with feminism, as well as my occupation. I was always hoping to find stories of women professors, but such stories did not begin to appear until I no longer needed them, until I had tenure and knew enough answers to get by. Nonetheless, as a reader of *Professorromane*, I've been sharply aware of the women who appear in the background, as students, as eccentric dons and dames, and especially as faculty wives. This book is dedicated to them.

chapter 1

The Fifties

IVORY TOWERS

THE ACADEMIC NOVELS of the 1950s depict a society with its own rules and traditions, cut off from the outside world, a snug, womblike, and, for some, suffocating world. But in contrast to those that would follow, they deal with large communal units, the college, the faculty, the university, rather than a single department. The professor's loyalty is to this large institution.

The decade began with one of the most reverent, idyllic, and utopian academic novels ever written—C. P. Snow's *The Masters* (1951). A large part of its appeal is Snow's conviction that the life of an Oxbridge don is one of the happiest and most significant a man can lead. In his appendix, "Reflections on the College Past," Snow comments, in the voice of his narrator Lewis Eliot, that "everyone, inside and out, took it for granted that the academic life was a valuable one to live." Any individual subject to doubts is reassured and sustained by living within the community, and "for many it was a profound comfort to be one of a society completely sure of itself, completely certain of its values, completely without misgivings about whether it was living a good life." Indeed, Eliot concludes, although he had "moved about a good deal among the layers of society, and . . . had the luck to live intimately among half a dozen different vocations," among all of these, "the college was the place where men lived the least anxious, the most comforting, the freest lives."[1]

On the other hand, the '50s also produced the funniest academic satire of the century, Kingsley Amis's *Lucky Jim*, set in a provincial redbrick university. The book portrays professors as stuffy, ridiculous phoneys, whose confidence is complacency and whose self-importance is matched only by their insignificance. In *The Modern British Novel*, Malcolm Bradbury describes *Lucky Jim* as "the exemplary Fifties novel. The story of Jim Dixon, the young history lecturer in a provincial university who is inwardly and comically at odds with the Bloomsburified academic, artistic and social culture of his elders, captured a powerful contemporary mood."[2] David Lodge, who read *Lucky Jim* in 1955 "with exquisite pleasure" when he finished his degree at University College, London, and who was "deeply indebted" to its example, recalls that "to many young people who grew up in the post-war period, and benefited from the 1944 Education Act, it seemed that the old pre-war upper classes still maintained their privileged position because they commanded the social and cultural high ground." Jim Dixon is "taking up a university post at a time when provincial universities were all mini-Oxbridges, aping and largely staffed by graduates of the ancient universities."[3] Jim has no patience with the pretensions and artiness of his colleagues; in the novel's climax he denounces them publicly—"the homemade pottery crowd, the organic husbandry crowd, the recorder-playing crowd," the "bloody Mozart" crowd of snobs and fools—and he leaves for the larger world with a great burst of anarchic laughter.

The Masters takes place in an unnamed Cambridge college in January 1937, when Paul Jago, the senior tutor, tells the young law professor Lewis Eliot, the first-person and highly reliable narrator, that the master, Vernon Royce, has inoperable cancer. The main plot of the novel is the internal campaigning and election of a new master by the college's thirteen fellows, and the contest between Jago and the biologist Thomas Crawford for the position. The anonymity of the college makes it easier for academic readers to supply their own names and identify with their own departmental and university elections. Nevertheless, Snow admits in his Author's Note that his "fictional college stands upon an existing site, and its topography is similar to that of an existing college." Based mainly on Snow's own experiences at Christ's College, where he had been a graduate student and fellow, *The Masters* also has elements of Trinity College. Overall, as Janice Rossen notes, Cambridge in the 1930s is for Snow "the English university at its apotheosis," and John Halperin calls *The Masters* "the greatest academic novel ever written."[4]

Cambridge is very much a sanctuary, a snug, secure, and insulated place, where the dons are tucked up in their beds or served their meals by attentive servants, protected from the rough-and-tumble outside the walls. But at the same time, Snow was among the first to show the deadly serious and highly worldly machinations of university politics and their relation to the political machinations outside in an ugly dark decade. One of his symbols of the university's contradictions is the unheated monastic bedroom, bedchamber really, where Eliot sleeps under heaped blankets with snow coming in the windows—which "seemed like a curious example of the mixture of luxury and bizarre discomfort in which the college lived. Yet, in time, one missed the contrast between the warmth in bed and the frigid air one breathed, and it was not so easy to sleep elsewhere" (10).

Although he was primarily a scientist, Snow had written a book about Trollope, whom he admired chiefly for his ability to see his characters from the inside and the outside: "He could see a person as others saw him; he could also see him as he saw himself. He had both insight and empathy, working together in exceptional harmony."[5] In his own analysis of academic politics, Snow follows Trollope in his efforts to understand what motivates even the most crotchety or vain among the fellows, and although he has none of Trollope's humor, his detailed, sensitive portraits of the way these men function as scholars, as members of an academic community, as political animals, and as vulnerable human beings still stands as the best portrait of the academic type. Any academic reading the novel will encounter herself and many of her colleagues in these paradigmatic figures, who come from different fields, and whose ages range from twenty-four to eighty: the boy genius, the academic player, the campus politician, the radical, the embittered burned-out scholar, the affable manipulator, the social director, the contrarian spoiler, the elderly narcissist, the detached ironic observer. Ages and generations are very important to Snow; they form one of the social structures that underlie the obvious hierarchy of the college offices and interact with others, like fame, intellect, class, and wealth.

Jago, who is fifty, is ambitious to succeed Royce; he longs for the office and its perquisites, but Snow, or rather Lewis Eliot, describes these ambitions in a benign Shakespearean way as tragic flaws, rather than satirizing them as a lesser novelist would do.

In any society, he would have longed to be first; and he would have longed for it because of everything that marked him out as different from the rest. . . . He would love to hear himself called Master; he would love to begin a formal act at a college meeting, "I, Paul Jago, Master of the college. . . ." He wanted the grandeur of the Lodge, he wanted to be styled among the heads of houses. . . . Like most ambitious men, he believed that there were things that only he could do. . . . He had dreams of what he could do with his power. . . . With all his fervent ambition, he thought of a college peaceful, harmonious, gifted, creative, throbbing with joy and luminous with grace. (59–60)

Jago is a historian who has worked on the American Puritans, but he is no great scholar; he has an unfortunate marriage to a former pupil; and he is a conservative. Crawford, aged fifty-six, is a better scholar and a radical, with a hobby of military history and a concern for the Spanish civil war. But soon Eliot becomes a member of the Jago party; Jago's campaign managers are officers of the college, the two men who "run things." Charles Chrystal, the dean, forty-eight, sits on the university Senate and is always being appointed to committees. No scholar—"still a first-rate teacher, but he had done nothing original" (29)—Chrystal has made a happy life for himself as a "power in the college," the man behind the throne; and he is also "drawn to success and power on the grand scale" (15). Arthur Brown, forty-six, another historian—he "wrote an intricate account of the diplomatic origins of the Crimean War soon after he graduated, and then stopped" (29)—is the Second Tutor and would be in for a promotion if Jago got the Mastership. So neither Chrystal nor Brown is a major scholar, but "they knew how men in a college behaved, and the different places in which each man was weak, ignorant, indifferent, obstinate, or strong. They never overplayed their hand; they knew just how to take the opinion of the college after they had settled a question in private" (29). Neither are they greedy or ambitious; they are loyal to the college and to help it makes them feel as if they serve "a purpose outside themselves" (30). They are happy to work behind the scenes, whereas Jago is eager for "all the trappings, titles, ornaments, and show of power"(59).

Throughout the novel, Eliot, Chrystal, and Brown attempt to sway or seduce the other fellows into voting a majority for Jago.

Among those they have to confront is the prickly bursar, Godfrey Winslow, independently wealthy, with a "savage temper and rude tongue" (18). A classicist, he has published nothing, but he has some small power that he uses in quarrels with his colleagues and sniping at their work. Winslow's soft spot is his son, an athlete who is preparing for the history tripos under Brown's supervision. If Winslow Junior can manage a third, he may "stand a chance of the colonial service" (22). Then there is Ronald Nightingale, forty-three, a bachelor, a teetotaler, and a resentful and unhappy man. "He had once possessed great promise. He had known what it was to hold creative dreams: and they had not come off." A brilliant theoretical chemist, Nightingale burned out young and as a result has been corroded with envy. "Each job in the college for which he was passed over, he saw with intense suspicion as a sign of the conspiracy directed against him. His reputation in his subject was already gone. He would not get into the Royal Society now. But, as March came round each year, he waited for the announcement of the Royal elections in expectation, in anguish, in bitter suspiciousness, at moments in the knowledge of what he might have been" (44). Nightingale will trade his vote for a promise of being made a college officer.

Francis Getliffe, Eliot's best friend, thirty-four, is a gifted scientist, working secretly on the origins of radar for the Air Ministry. The most politically radical of the fellows, he worries that conservatives like Jago will "either let us drift lock, stock, and barrel to the Fascists; or they'll get us into a war which we shall be bloody lucky not to lose" (69). Roy Calvert, twenty-seven, the college's most brilliant hope, is an Orientalist and linguist who already has that greatest of all academic distinctions, an international reputation. Calvert is almost Maileresque in his attitudes toward research: "It's like making love—suddenly your unconscious takes control. And nothing can stop you. You know that you're making old Mother Nature sit up and beg. And you say to her, 'I've got you where I want you, you old bitch'" (295). No wonder that Royce's daughter Joan is desperately in love with him; he is the glamour boy, the one compared to Ibsen's visionary scholar Eilert Lovberg, "with vine-leaves in his hair." But like Lovberg, he is also prone to bouts of severe, almost suicidal, depression.

Calvert and Walter Luke, only twenty-four, are junior faculty members, without tenure or "permanency," and somewhat more vulnerable to college politics, although not as insecure as contemporary junior untenured faculty or redbrick lecturers like Lucky Jim Dixon. Among the older fellows, the master's deputy, mathematician Despard-Smith, has turned to drink at seventy: "I've had a disappointing life, Eliot. . . . I've not been given the recognition I had a right to expect" (290). He would have liked to have been master himself and sadistically enjoys watching Jago's ups and downs.

Eustace Pilbrow, seventy-four, is the most loved of the fellows, detested only by Nightingale. He works on literature, classic and modern, and has published books on the Latin novelists; he travels incessantly and is at ease in the contemporary world of art and letters, praising some "Central European he had just discovered, who would be a great writer in ten years" and "bringing persecuted artists to England, and spending most of his income on them" (65). Pilbrow "was eccentric, an amateur, a connoisseur; he spent much of his time abroad, but he was intensely English, he could not have been anything else but English. He belonged to the fine flower of the peaceful nineteenth century. A great war had not shattered his feeling, gentlemanly and unselfconscious, that one went where one wanted and did what one liked" (65).

Maurice Gay, eighty and the oldest of the fellows, is a scholar of the Icelandic sagas. Snow satirizes his narcissicism but basically honors what he does.

> He was not a clever man. . . . He was simple, exuberantly vain, as pleased with himself as a schoolboy who had just received a prize. But he had enormous zest and gusto, unbounded delight in his work. He had enjoyed every minute of his researches. Somehow all his vitality, mental and physical, had poured into them without constraint or inhibition or self-criticism. He did not trouble himself; he had not the equipment to begin, with the profound whys of existence—but in his line he had a strong simple unresting imagination. (261)

Gay is an early version of the crossover academic, who also can write for a general audience and has made a lot of money from his books. "I will give you young men a piece of advice" he says cheerfully. "Satisfy the scholars first. Show them that you're better than any of them, that's the thing to do. But when you've become an authority, don't neglect your public. Why, I should welcome my books being presented by the films" (259).

How will these men choose a master, with all the term implies of hierarchy and power? Snow's analysis of their motives is subtle and psychologically complex. Above all, he understands the erotics of rivalry, what Eve Sedgwick has interpreted as the structures of triangular and homosocial desire. Jago and Crawford are oddly bound by desiring the same thing; in a way, in this very repressed male society, they desire each other: "It was not the first time I had noticed the electric attraction of rivalry: rivals, whether competing for a job, opposing each other in politics, struggling for the same woman, are for mysterious moments closer than any friends" (158). He is surprising and instructive in his understanding of something irrational, primal, and contradictory in a contest: "There are some hidden streaks in any politics, which only flash to the surface in an intense election such as this. Suddenly they leap out: one finds to one's astonishment that there are moments when one loves one's rival—despises one's supporters—hates one's candidate" (198). This unconscious element in politics drives the outcome of the election, and Snow analyzes it usefully for anyone involved in academic negotation, decision making, and choice. After a certain point, there is a switch in attachments, perhaps because the "leader" is so demanding, so exhausting, so melodramatic, so egotistical, whereas the opponent has the charm of modesty and mystery. "I saw men as tough and dominating as Chrystal," Eliot observes, "entangled in compromise and in time hypnotized by their own technique: believing that they were being sensible and realistic, taking their steps for coherent practical reasons, while in fact they were moved by vacillations which they did not begin to understand. I saw men enjoying forming coalitions, just as Chrystal did, and revelling in the contact with their opponents. I saw the same impulse to change sides, to resent one's leader and become fascinated by one's chief opponent" (302).

The novel ends with the election of Crawford and the defeat of Jago, who is deeply shamed in ways that reflect the claustrophobia of the secure institution: "When will the news go round the university? Has it got outside the college yet? Who would be the first of his enemies to laugh?" (309). In a closed society, defeat is never forgotten; old quarrels, old contests are still painfully alive. Defeats and losses would not be so painful if no one knew about them, or at least no one you knew; so within the college they are magnified and multiplied. That's the worm in the Oxbridge apple. And the great irony of academic life is that while no one else, perhaps, may be aware of how graciously or meanly the loser plays his part, the loser is obsessed, suffused with consciousness of it. "I shall have to watch another man in the place I should have filled," Jago cries. "I shall have to call him Master" (309).

The public moment of his surrender takes place in the combination room after a dinner in hall, with decanters and silver, "a pile of peaches in a great silver dish" (330). Jago does well; he invites Crawford to dinner—pauses and chokes out the word *Master*, and then slips away early from the dinner in silence. The scene is a particularly overt and explicit demonstration of academic hierarchy and public submission, echoed in the fictional pen ceremony in the movie *A Beautiful Mind*. When the great mathematical genius John Nash lunches at the Princeton faculty club, the other professors, one by one, approach and lay their fountain pens before him—pure phallic obeisance.

How accurate a picture of Cambridge life was *The Masters*? Snow's contemporaries and colleagues maintained that it was very inaccurate indeed. Even Charles Raven, the theologian who was the model for Jago, declared that Snow did not understand the academic life: "Sir Charles offers us only careerism. That is the case against him."[6] When I first visited Cambridge with my husband as an awed young faculty wife in the 1960s, we dined at Trinity College High Table as the guests of Professor Ralph Leigh, and I noted the evening's impressive menu in the yellowing margins of my paperback copy of Virginia Woolf's *A Room of One's Own*: chef's salad, chicken Washington, new potatoes and peas, Trinity College burnt cream, savory crab on toast, followed by port, madeira, sauterne, claret, biscuits, cheese, fresh peaches, coffee and cigars, brandy and seltzer. (How anyone did any work after such a meal is still a mystery to me. Maybe there is something to be said for the abstemious prunes and custard Woolf dined upon at Girton.)

At dinner I was seated next to the great Victorian historian George Kitson-Clark, on whose work I had recently been examined for my Ph.D. He was none too responsive to my eager questions (I didn't know that it was taboo to discuss one's work at dinner), but he perked up when the pudding arrived—Trinity College burnt cream, or crème brûlée, and he enthusiastically showed me how to whack the sugar crust with a huge silver spoon like the one wielded by the duchess in Alice in Wonderland. The economist Rab Butler, who had barely missed being prime minister, was the master of Trinity, and in the private dining room, after dinner, with portraits of alumni like Dryden and Wordsworth, I asked Ralph Leigh whether Cambridge at all resembled Snow's portrait. "Not at all, absolutely not," he replied. "Much exaggerated, out of date, quite absurd." A few minutes later, as Butler circulated the decanters of port and claret, I noticed a frisson at the table, and Leigh hissed into my ear, "The fool is passing the port the wrong way round!" Snow must have had something right.

Like many authors of academic fiction who would come after him, Snow insisted that his book was fictional and points out that there have been no actual elections of masters at Cambridge in recent times. But he admitted that there had been some close ones in the past and "a well-authenticated" case of "a last-minute change of fortune" in the memoirs of Mark Pattison. Pattison was the rector of Lincoln College, Oxford, in George Eliot's day, and indeed some of his contemporaries thought he was the model for Casaubon. That debate goes on, but certainly Pattison was defeated in his first election to the rectorship of Lincoln in 1851 and wrote in his journal of his devastation: "My new-cut ambition was dashed to the ground. . . . A blank, dumb despair filled me, a chronic heartache took possession of me, perceptible even through sleep."[7] Minor though it may be in the eyes of the outside world, especially in 1937, on the brink of World War II, a college election can be a matter of tragic intensity to its candidates.

Unlike the academic novelists who followed him, Snow was deliberately writing a historical novel. His vision of the university is an idealized view of an irrecuperable past. The thirteen fellows include about half who are, in some ways, failures or frauds; but Snow seems to admire the college for providing a society where they can thrive. As they gather around the high table, they bring to mind the mystical fellowship of the knights of the Round Table or even the twelve Apostles. It is a valid criticism that Snow focuses on careerism; the functions of the university in the broader society are largely ignored,

both in research and in teaching. He is obviously aware of the contrast between the rationality these men aspire to by vocation and the
all-too-human passions and pettinesses they lapse into. Yet he remains convinced of the value of the ideal, celebrates it in his novel,
and implies that the university comes close to realizing it. He is just
about the last writer to do so and so looks steadily into the past even
as he lays the groundwork for the genre.

Kingsley Amis's view of the university in *Lucky Jim* (1954) could
scarcely be more different from Snow's. If Cambridge dons were the
masters, the burdened lecturers at the new redbricks were the servants. Whereas the old Norse scholar Gay is the revered sage of *The
Masters*, the spirit of a heroic past, Amis despised Anglo-Saxon epics
and the vision of life they preached. In a letter he wrote as a student,
he raged against the Old English requirement at Oxford: "The war-
riors and broken-down retainers who strut bawling across the its
pages repel by their childish fits of self-glorification and self-pity. The
cheapest contemporary novel has more to teach us than these painful
reminders of what we have long outgrown."[8] Jim Dixon's outburst
against the trumped-up values of "Merrie England" reflects Amis's
preferences.

Moreover, whereas *The Masters* is about staying on forever, *Lucky
Jim* is about moving on. Whereas the masters are sure that they are
at the very center of the universe, Jim is suffused with longing for a
world elsewhere. And it is definitely not the world of Oxbridge. He
has a recurring "visual image that had haunted him ever since he
took on this job. He seemed to be looking from a darkened room
across a darkened back street to where, against a dimly-glowing
evening sky, a small line of chimney-pots stood out as if carved from
tin. . . . He was certain it was the image of London, and just as
certain that it wasn't any part of London he had ever visited."[9] Jim
wants to be in the city, in a magical London that is the opposite of
the university, and he does finally leave, in a triumphantly comic
conclusion. Just as *The Masters* appeals to and addresses that side of
the academic psyche that idealizes the ivory tower, *Lucky Jim* speaks
to the academic spirit of rebellion and impatience, the feeling that
life must be lived more intensely outside the walls. "It is no accident," Janice Rossen notes, "that many of the best University novels
are about someone leaving academe at the end of the book."[10]

And while Snow's world sublimates sexual energy in male power games, Amis is much more interested in sex itself. Malcolm Bradbury wrote a funny parody of Snow and Amis called "An Extravagant Fondness for the Love of Women," imagining Jim Dixon at Cambridge. Lewis Eliot holds forth on the young Dixon's perverse lack of interest in their collegiate political machinations: "He struck me oddly, as a man curiously uninterested in power. Jago told me that he had seen in him an extravagant fondness for the love of women, and it was probably this propensity that curbed his natural instincts. He had avoided our cabals, remained unspeaking during our gossip, and taken a negligible part in our recent poisoning attempt upon the Provost." Dixon seems much more interested in hanging around with barmaids; but Eliot is philosophical: "It was, however, hardly my business to warn or to criticize; and in any case, if a man is not prepared to accept and take on his own terms every Fellow of the college, he is hardly likely to acquire enough material for a *roman-fleuve*."[11]

Amis had recognized the potential of the provincial university as a comic setting in 1946, when he visited his friend Philip Larkin at Leicester University, where Larkin was working as a librarian. They went into the Senior Common room, and Amis instantly saw it as a cultural microcosm, the setting for a new kind of novel: "I looked around a couple of times and said to myself, 'Christ, somebody ought to do something with this.' Not that it was awful—well, only a bit; it was strong and sort of *developed*, a whole mode of existence no one had got onto from the outside, like the SS in 1940, say."[12] I love the outrageousness of that simile—the spirit of the faculty, not really awful but sort of fascist. His own experience as a young faculty member at Swansea reinforced this early impression, although in many ways he enjoyed teaching and liked his colleagues. In particular, he had scant regard for the male academic community as a model. Amis had been an undergraduate at Oxford at the time when J. R. R. Tolkien, C. S. Lewis, and their fellow "Inklings" "met in a pub across the road from Amis's college for hearty male conversation . . . gatherings to which no woman was ever admitted."[13] But Amis detested such "hearty male" gatherings of men he regarded as the driest and most tediously donnish of the university set—his mocking codename for Tolkien in his letters to Larkin was Professor Bollkeen.

Part of what makes *Lucky Jim* seem contemporary is the presence of women on the faculty. On the other hand, they are pretty dreadful. Margaret Peel is a lecturer in history and a classic arty bluestocking type. Jim says a lot about her taste in clothes—"the green Paisley frock in combination with the low-heeled quasi-velvet shoes," the "multi-colored shirt, skirt with fringed hem and pocket," wooden beads, a brooch of the wooden letter M, or a quadruple string of pearls with her royal-blue taffeta party dress with a bow. Although she has a sort of "minimal prettiness" (108), she wears too much makeup and gets lipstick on her teeth. She laughs self-consciously, with the tinkle of silver bells. Margaret desperately needs a makeover; it's easy to sympathize with her, although Amis works hard to turn us against her.

Margaret is an academic neurotic, always shown from the outside, who tries to pressure men through guilt into romantic entanglements; but there are signs even to Jim of how tense and unhappy she is. He notes her thin jaw, the prominent tendons in her neck, "the tufts of brown hair that overhung the earpieces of her glasses . . . the faint but unmistakable downward curve of the mouth" (22). Yet Jim leads her on, gives her a book of poems with something affectionate written on the flyleaf. He tries to screw her. When he finally breaks off with her, he thinks, "What a pity it was . . . that she wasn't better-looking, that she didn't read the articles in the three-halfpenny press that told you which colour lipstick went with which natural colouring. With twenty percent more of what she lacked in these ways she'd never have run into any of her appalling difficulties: the vices and morbidities born of loneliness would have remained safely dormant until old age" (168). The plight of the female lecturer, one feels, is even worse than that of the angry young man.

Jim is in no sense a scholar and has none of the passion that drives Snow's dons. His special subject is "Medieval Life and Culture," but he is a medievalist because it was the "soft option" at Leicester. "Haven't you noticed," he ruminates, "how we all specialize in what we hate most?" (33–34). So he is stuck with what Margaret pretentiously calls "the Middle Age" (87). Unlike the dedicated and boastful dons of *The Masters*, Dixon has only shame for his own "scholarship": "the amount of frenzied fact-grubbing and fanatical boredom that had gone into it" (15). In the book's most famous scene, he is forced to summarize his unpublished article "The Economic Influence of the Developments in Shipbuilding Techniques, 1450 to 1485" ("it was a perfect title, in that it crystallized the article's niggling mindlessness, its funereal parade of yawn-enforcing facts, the pseudo-light it threw upon non-problems"), which begins "this strangely neglected topic," a phrase that has become self-mocking academic shorthand for any contrived, tedious, irrelevant piece of obscure pedantry we feel compelled to produce.

But Jim is not ignorant or anti-intellectual. He tells London industrialist Gore-Urquhart, his mentor and eventual employer, "Well taught and sensibly taught, history could do people a hell of a lot of good. But in practice it doesn't work out like that. Things get in the way. I don't quite see who's to blame for it. Bad teaching's the main thing" (218). In the movie version of *Lucky Jim*, Dixon has become the campus hero, the most popular lecturer on campus, whose students applaud his candid and courageous denunciations of cant. But that is a new form of idealization, the young united in their revolt against stifling tradition. In the novel, Jim's triumph is mostly private; he has the last laugh as he leaves for London, but no one at the college shares it.

Philip Larkin, to whom *Lucky Jim* is dedicated, also tried his hand at an academic satire, but his protagonist has none of Jim's bounce. The unfinished draft was published posthumously as "A New World Symphony." A miserable lecturer, Butterfield is applying for a Chair on a "dull, windy Sunday afternoon," in a room with a "sluggish fire" and faded wallpaper. He has to drink a bottle of Scotch to sustain his courage; "on this Sunday he was due to launch himself at the last crag, the summit, of his life. If he gained it, his life, he felt, would be a success; if not, a failure." But Butterfield knows that his application and his C.V. are not up to snuff. "He tried imagining what (in a successful application) should come next: Assistant Lecturer 1923–26: Lecturer 1926–1929: Fiddle Reader in Godknowswhat at, probably, Manchester, 1929–1930: Assistant Professor, Idaho State University, 1930–1933: Faddle Lecturer on the Seventeenth Century, University of Oxford 1934–1939: Work of national importance (Ministry of Education) 1939–1945: three years spent finishing off a commissioned definitive edition of someone or other: publications include. . . .

His own imagination unsteadied him, and he poured out another glass. It was hopeless, hopeless, hopeless."[14] It's *The Masters* as told by Eeyore.

The best American academic novel of the 1950s was *The Groves of Academe*, by Mary McCarthy, published in 1952. McCarthy had some experience with college teaching; she had taught at tiny Bard (only 80 students) in 1945, where she supervised seven students in addition to doing a course on the Russian novel and one on the modern novel, which began with Jane Austen. She had her seven-year-old son, Reuel, with her; perhaps that is why there are families and children and baby-sitters living on her fictional campus.[15]

McCarthy said that she had invented her fictional college nonetheless: "I had taught at Bard College and Sarah Lawrence, but I didn't want to make a composite of those two places. I really wanted to make a weird imaginary college of my own. I even took a trip to the Mennonite country in Pennsylvania to try to find a perfect location for it. . . . it was Lititz, Pennsylvania, the home of the pretzel. There's a very charming old-fashioned sort of academy, a girls' college, there." The novel is set at Jocelyn, a small progressive college, founded in the late 1930s by "an experimental educator and lecturer . . . who wished to strike a middle course between the existing extremes, between Aquinas and Dewey, the modern dance and the labor movement." This enterprise is funded by a coalition of rich society ladies, who want "a center of 'personalized' education, with courses tailored to the individual need, like their own foundation-garments, and a staff of experts and consultants, each with a little 'name' in his field, like the Michaels and Antoines of Fifth Avenue, to interpret the student's personality" (59).

With its emphasis on progressive education and its setting during the McCarthy (no relation) witchhunts of the '50s, *The Groves of Academe* is very American. Mary McCarthy had gone to Vassar and took women professors for granted, and in her book she presents several feisty ones. Ivy Legendre, the lesbian head of the theatre department, declares about the traditional winter break, "I don't care what you call it, Faculty Rest or Florida Special . . . but get the little bastards out of my yellow hair." Alma Fortune, who had been a New Woman "of the *femme savante* school," dresses in jerseys with necklaces of turquoise and Mexican silver, smokes "little Cuban cheroots" (99), and, despite having been married, suffers from "all the usual disorders of the repressed female brain-worker" (105).

Above all, there is the incomparable Domna Rejnev, the youngest member of the literature department, only twenty-three, from Radcliffe; beautiful, with skin "the color of old piano keys" and lips that are naturally rose. As brilliant and ardent as a George Eliot heroine, she loves the challenge of supervising an enormous range of independent studies: "To be allowed, under the cover of duty, to pursue the world's history down its recondite by-ways was, for Domna Rejnev, a pure nightly joy, a passion of legitimate conquest, and her students were quick to discover that they could not please Miss Rejnev better than by discovering a wish to study an author she had not read, preferably an old author, in some forgotten cranny of culture" (74). Domna Rejnev was my role model not only for being a teacher but also for being a student, and my poor advisors at Bryn Mawr had to read papers on Baron Corvo and Sheridan LeFanu.

McCarthy has explained that *The Groves of Academe* "started with the plot." A Dickensian humbug of a professor, Henry Mulcahy, loses his job at Jocelyn and spreads the rumor that he is being fired because he was once a member of the Communist Party, knowing that the college and its faculty are too politically correct (to use a term that became ubiquitous a decade later) to be seen as persecuting the Left. "The plot and this figure: there can't be the plot without this figure of the impossible individual, the unemployable professor and his campaign for justice," said McCarthy. "Justice, but in quotes, you know, and serious in a way. What is justice for the unemployable person? That was conceived from the beginning as a plot: the whole idea of the reversal at the end, when Mulcahy is triumphant and the President is about to lose his job or quit, when the worm turns and is triumphant. I didn't see exactly what would happen in between; the more minute details weren't worked out. But I did see that there would be his campaign for reinstatement; and then his secret would be discovered. In this case that he had *not* been a Communist."[16] Domna and her faculty friends fight for his reinstatement, although they become increasingly uneasy about his lying and manipulation.

Mulcahy's duplicity is revealed at a campus poetry conference, which becomes the source of all kinds of collegiate quarrels. First, the faculty fight over which poets will be invited. "As with all symposia and anthologies, criticism fastened on omissions. It was claimed that certain allegedly leading figures had not been invited" (197). A notice goes up on the bulletin board: "WHERE ARE THE POETS OF THE MASSES?" (197). Rumors spread that the conference is a set-up for cruel confrontation between generations, and indignities to elderly poets" (198). Domna asks why no women have been invited, and one is added at the last minute. Then they squabble over the entertainment: "already, of course, there was great rivalry over where they were to stay, who was to give the dinner for them, who cocktails, and so on" (188).

Naturally, the conference is a debacle, a series of confrontations, and the authentic poet of the masses, summoned to the president's office, reveals that "the bird Mulcahy was never in the Party or near it" (245). But in a clever twist, this proves to be Mulcahy's victory. He can claim that he was spied upon, threaten to write to the American Association of University Professors, and bring a lawsuit for political harassment. And finally, the president of the college gives up and resigns: "The college would never get rid of him as long as I was at the tiller. With another skipper, who can't be blackmailed, there's a fair chance of getting him out" (254).

Amazingly ahead of its time, *The Groves of Academe* is bracingly cynical and worldly-wise without condemning higher education, liberals, or intellectuals. With the exception of the repellent and unctuous Mulcahy, the faculty are motivated by the highest ideals, and they share a genuine community of learning. McCarthy simply can't be pious or preachy about them. Today, says Sanford Pinsker, "a contemporary counterpart of Mulcahy's, equally threatened by an impending pink slip, might consider giving over one of his classes—say, a semester before the ax is scheduled to fall—to an announcement that he no longer wants to keep his sexual lifestyle hidden inside the closet."[17] Indeed, this plot has been done in the French movie *Le Placard*, with Daniel Auteuil getting his clerical job back when he pretends to be gay. And the correctness McCarthy so presciently mocked has evolved from political to a broad social dogmatism.

In contrast to the sparkling and evergreen *Groves*, Randall Jarrell's *Pictures from an Institution* (1954), which some literary critics profess to admire, strikes me as tedious and almost unreadable. Dedicated to Mary McCarthy and Hannah Arendt, *Pictures* goes through a year at Benton, a progressive women's college, at which a malignant woman novelist and her meek husband skewer the faculty in a series of acid portraits. In the spring of 1951, Jarrell told Hannah Arendt that he had written a "prose book" inspired by her *Origins of Totalitarianism* (he would later disguise *Pictures* by draping it with a dust jacket from her book), and the idea behind the rather plotless work seems to be that a small liberal arts college resembles a totalitarian society. He had read *The Groves of Academe*, but his novel was very different, writes William Pritchard, tending "toward brilliant one-liners that obliterated 'responsible' analysis of his subject"; Jarrell's "writing seems to exist mainly for the purpose of outdoing itself, as each sentence takes off with the ambition of going its predecessor one better."[18]

Frankly, I prefer Carlos Baker's sentimental *A Friend in Power* (1958), if only because it is about Princeton. Baker, a professor of English at Princeton who died in 1987, was the biographer and great critic of Hemingway. He was a World War II veteran and a crew-cut image of the American male. His first novel, *A Friend in Power* is often described as an American version of *The Masters*. Set at Enfield University, it describes through the consciousness of French professor Edward Tyler the internal search for a new president to replace the longtimer Homer Vaughn, who has resigned. Like Snow, Baker is an unquestioning subscriber to the higher ideals of academic life; his university also separates the insiders, the Enfielders, from the outsiders, the outfielders.

Based on the search process that appointed Robert Goheen, then a young assistant professor of classics, to the Princeton presidency in 1956, after the long reign of President Harold Dodds, *A Friend in Power* gives a thinly disguised and much-romanticized picture of Princeton in the 1950s, a blandly suburban but idyllic Princeton where there is no political dissent, no intellectual fervor, and no female interference. (Edward Said gives a much harsher view of Princeton in the '50s in his memoir *Out of Place*, describing it as "a provincial, small-minded college," anti-intellectually sedate, racially homogeneous, "unpolitical, self-satisfied, and oblivious" [19].) Wives, good or bad, for the faculty, and prostitutes for the undergraduates provide the sexual element, but Baker sees no problem in this condition. At one point, Tyler sees a colleague with a strange woman in New York and speculates that she must be "some female biology professor from one of the women's colleges in New York."[20]

Baker's title comes from a comment by Henry Adams: "A friend in power is a friend lost." The loss is not to people but to scholarship, and Baker focuses on the conflict between the quiet life of research and the call to (unwanted) public service, rather than the siren call of ambition and power. The scholar who unwillingly becomes president, Edward Tyler, is on the search committee for the new president, along with two scientists, two social scientists, and another humanist. What Tyler really wants is a Guggenheim Fellowship, so he can finish his book on Voltaire. Like *The Masters*, *A Friend in Power* ends with Tyler humbly accepting the mantle of authority and literally picking up his jacket as he puts the pages of his unfinished masterpiece into the drawer.

Tyler actually does some teaching and reads some student papers as well. He wrestles mightily with his lecture preparation:

> Today he would deal with satire and irony, try to demonstrate the multiple profundities of Montesquieu in the *Lettres Persanes*. Out of these notes—these pencil-scrawls, these patches of typing with their interlineations, these scribbled marginalia, these afterthoughts which had become forethoughts, these forethoughts that became afterthoughts—would have to come the urbane and finished product. The notes were the rough quarry from which he must extract the block of marble. And then this mass, to be worked over for fifty minutes, to be carved with words into the proportioned statue, the Galatea. And finally, hardest of all, this statue to be brought alive by any verbal magic he could muster. Not only brought alive but borne alive into the heads (and if possible the hearts) of those four dozen yawning, alert, scratching, attentive, surreptitiously-*Eagle*-reading, argumentative, girl-dreaming, out-of-window-gazing undergraduates who would straggle in to take their places when the chapel-bell struck eleven. (62)

Teaching—or more accurately, performing, reciting, and lecturing—at Enfield is so noble and memorable and ego-involving a task that in one of the novel's subplots, an aged alcoholic emeritus runs away from his minder in New York City and turns up at the Enfield Inn claiming that he has been invited by the department to give some lectures: "Poor old Alcide. In the old man's mind some foggy vision of a lecture-hall, crammed with students and faculty, great applause as he stood up, hushed attention as he spoke, laughter at the Gallic jokes, the finespun witticisms. . . . The composite memory of a hundred such lectures swimming and merging now in the old brain" (97). What's striking in retrospect is how familiar and how alien this is—how distant is the showpiece lecture from the heads and hearts of the undergraduates, and how enormous is the gap between lecturing, applause, and learning. These gentlemanly lords of the lecture would have been shocked at being asked how they assessed what their students had learned and how many of their students had learned it. And shocked still more had the assessment been done and they had seen the results.

But high-minded passages like these are intended to demonstrate that Tyler is the man the committee has in mind when it defines its presidential goals: "a broad-ranging mind, absolute integrity, nobility of motives. A deep concern, of course, for the welfare of liberal education. The kind of man the alumni would respect. A man without ambitions on the national scene. A man of settled religious convictions. He should be adaptable to a variety of situations, and should have a capacity for back-breaking work. . . . He must be absolutely devoted to the two great tasks of the university: the education of young men and the extension of the boundaries of knowledge" (69). Neither Baker nor his model, Robert Goheen, could possibly have imagined just how adaptable a university president would need to be in the next decade.

Unlike Snow, who grasps the psychology of rivalry in a small community, Baker does not explore the effects of power on male friendships, and indeed, apart from a Hemingwayesque fishing trip Tyler takes with a colleague, there is not much male friendship or bonding in the book. But the Princeton lore is lovingly managed. Baker describes the faculty meeting room: "Ionian white and gold, dignified but not gaudy, rich with polished furniture, the maroon plush on the seats worn as threadbare as the faculty's pants, the faculty room was only . . . half filled. In the attitudes of some old painting

. . . the faculty sat, white-haired, gray-haired, brown or black or blond or bald, in the mahogany seats which ranged like elongated pews down either side to the room's focal point" (7–8). It still looks like that. Moreover, the seating plan still holds: "Across the room sat the usual battery of social scientists, natural scientists, and engineers. . . . On his own side—such was the unwritten custom—sat the literary people, the historians and philosophers, the art-historians and musicologists. They faced the scientific brethren on the opposing side as by symbolic intent" (9).

Humanists to the left, scientists to the right—that was one way of thinking about the faculty meeting of the '50s. In most of the academic novels of the decade, however, that opposition was purely intellectual; both sides, whether in Snow's English college or in Baker's American university, felt united in their endeavor. Even in McCarthy's college, one's sympathies lie with the well-intentioned president and faculty who are victimized by the unscrupulous upstart. In that respect, Amis's *Lucky Jim* is the source of most of the academic novels that followed, the real origin of the genre, for Jim Dixon is the author's vehicle for an attack on a dying tradition and a suffocating institution.

chapter 2

❧

The Sixties

TRIBAL TOWERS

THE 1960S WERE A turbulent decade, but not in the pages of the academic novel. Political protest, the Vietnam War, the civil rights movement, the women's movement, Stonewall, the sexual revolution, the drug culture, the growth of rock music and popular culture, all the things that were changing my life as a graduate student and instructor in the '60s, are absent from the fiction of the decade. Of course, the novel is always a belated form of social commentary; just as the academic novel of the '50s was really about the disruptive postwar generation of the '40s, the books that came out in the '60s looked back to the previous more placid decade. And yet there is and was something disturbing about the disconnnect between the books and life of the '60s. These novels do register a lot of unhappiness, protest, and discontent. Women particularly figure as angry and excluded. Yet these rumbles are stifled and stilled. Novel after novel ends in weak compromise, or simply business-as-usual; the rebels aren't even punished or banished; they just learn to love Big Brother or to fake their love convincingly.

Within these novels, there's a shift of focus from the university or the Oxbridge college to the American English department, which begins to be the place where protest is voiced, and the tone certainly shifts from the admiring tones of Snow to a much more acerbic view of academic life and a much more Darwinian sense of the university and the struggle for survival. The department is portrayed as an ethnographic entity, a tribe.

Within this tribal culture, novelists begin to explore the Freudian subtexts of department life, especially the Oedipal projections on to the chair, or at least the alpha male, who is the father who must be emulated by the men and served by the women. The beloved master of Snow's Cambridge and Baker's Enfield has given way to the terrifying senior professor, the castrating department chair, and the formidable patriarchal critic. Sometimes the abusive father can be overthrown, but even so, the death of the father is traumatic for all the sons, and guilt-inducing for the daughters. The chair's Oedipal role comes with the territory, independent of the occupant's personality. For female chairs, virtually unrepresented in academic fiction except as murder victims, the parallel would be the role of the Mother, much more difficult, because the mother's authority is always resented while her nurturance is in much more demand. But in the '60s, the rare female professor is ambivalent about power and in denial about ambition. Female characters are generally seductive students or frustrated faculty wives.

One of the most caustic, vituperative, and antifeminist novels of the decade is John W. Aldridge's *The Party at Cranton* (1960). Aldridge had taught at the University of Vermont from 1948 to 1955, and then at Sarah Lawrence. He eventually became professor of English at New York University. In 1953 and 1954, Aldridge had also lectured in the celebrated and august Christian Gauss Seminars in Criticism at Princeton, founded and run by the formidable critic Richard Blackmur, who directed Princeton's creative writing program. Cranton is all too recognizably Princeton, a WASP-y suburb and the home of the Gallup Polls, a place where there were so many "facilities for the tasteful pursuit of the good life" that "the facilities for mere life had almost been crowded out of town, and one sometimes had to travel miles just to buy a nail to put up the Daumier in the bathroom."[1]

Richard Waithe, a visiting scholar who narrates the story (he has held a fellowship to study Japanese translation of James Joyce), mocks Cranton's pseudosocial life: "Cranton parties . . . were so strictly regulated by the rules of some complicated and secret code of etiquette that the people at them behaved as though they had all put on masks at the door and were engaged in playing a vastly esoteric game of charades" (17). Thus "it did not matter whether one attended a Cranton party every night for ten years or had been abroad ten years and suddenly returned: one was greeted in each case with the same show of professional cordiality, the same mechanical assurances that one was mechanically adored. Even if one saw the same people at parties night after night for those ten years, one got no nearer to them than one had been at the first party" (26).

We've all been to these parties, and probably even given some, but they are easy satirical targets. Waithe is such a bitchy narrator that the reader can't have much confidence that he would be a more genuine friend than his Cranton hosts. Moreover, while Aldridge's complaints about Princeton may sound closer to Edward Said than to Carlos Baker, the novel is less about snobbery, racism, and injustice than about Waithe's pique at his own marginality. Princeton has long been a popular setting for academic fiction, and, as Ann Waldron sums up in a review of "The Fictive Princeton," the portrait is not always bright. "In many novels about Princeton, . . . a dark narrative of class distinctions, regional snobbery, and antisemitism weaves in and out of the 'effusions.' Over and over, male authors have recounted the plight of the outsider at Princeton, and in their stories the outsider can be almost anybody—a midwesterner, a southerner, a westerner, a graduate of a public high school instead of a prep school, and, most outside of all, a Jew."[2] Waldron does not mention women—Princeton became coeducational in the early 1970s—but Aldridge is particularly cruel to the women on campus, both the harpyish faculty wives and the classicist Dorothy Murchison, who comes to give the Matilda Makepeace Willycombe lectures, and whom he portrays as a nymphomaniac, drunkard, and fraud.

Waithe reserves his sharpest barbs for Arthur Buchanan, the Blackmur figure. As the editor of a prestigious literary journal, Buchanan is the "godhead, or at the very least, head god" of the Cranton community, with the power to punish and reward; he resembles "a hugely complicated intellectual switchboard of obscure circuits and plugged-in connections reaching out to the farthest-flung precincts of the literary universe" (58). His acolytes believe that if they please him they will be rewarded with Guggenheim fellowships and if they offend him they will be cast out into darkness; and, like the academic tyrants who follow him in fiction, he enjoys teasing the powerless: "If ever he felt in imminent danger of being found out—as he very nearly had been once or twice—and of having one of his little pets go mad and fly at his throat, he would toss them from time to time a meaty bone from some old reputation which he had successfully reduced to carcass, and let them fall upon that and crunch it savagely between their long, sharp, angry teeth. That, as a rule, kept them quiet, for if there was one thing they like to worry and gnaw on . . . it was a reputation, old or new, tough or tender" (61).

The enslaved English professors of Cranton project all their pent-up rage onto literature itself. They produced criticism "the way other men might have beheaded dolls or stuck pins in effigies—with a viciousness almost ceremonial under the cold glare of the study lamp in the black of night. Criticism was their method of wreaking vengeance upon literature for being the one thing they could not succeed in by taking a degree or playing politics, and their resentment of it was boundless" (61–62). Aldridge also charges literary critics with what Harold Bloom would call the anxiety of influence. "Where they had once been sustained by the possibility of becoming great men, they now faced a situation in which it seemed taken for granted that all the great men had long since been. The solitary creation of literature had at some point given way to generalized criticism of it; it suddenly seemed more important to have read widely than to have written well" (101).

Finally, Aldridge translates the anxiety of the English department into blatantly sexual metaphors; at Cranton, all men are impotent except the writers and poets. Their castration is evident at the parties where their sexually frustrated wives gather hungrily around Buchanan. Yet Aldridge directs his most bitter attacks at the faculty wives. "It appeared to be always in their wives that the hostility came out" (62). Desperate for their husbands to succeed, the wives act out the covert hostility of their spouses. "If word got around at a party that a writer, especially a writer of reputation, was present, the claws of every young English instructor's wife in the room would come almost audibly unsheathed with a sound very much like the deadly whicker made by the released arrows of King Harry Olivier's gallant longbowmen at the start of the Battle of Agincourt, and a pack of fierce-eyed, grim-lipped Vassar and Smith graduates would converge on their victim, their sinewy bosoms swelling with blood lust" (63).

At the climactic Cranton party, Dorothy Murchison drunkenly accuses Buchanan of impotence and sexual sadism: "What's the *mat*ter,

Buchanan? Can't you get it up?" (163). There is a brawl and a scandal (at Princeton, stories about Blackmur's carryings-on, and the
time he bit a faculty wife at a party—oh, there were giants in those
days!—are still legend), but absolutely nothing happens: fade out.
Waithe is a wraith, and while he can witness to a scene, he cannot
create one of his own or act on his convictions.

In stark contrast to Aldridge is Alison Lurie's *Love and Friendship*
(1962), an academic novel written from the perspective of the highly
educated, sexually and intellectually frustrated faculty wife. Lurie
would later become the laureate of the unhappy faculty wife, in her
best-seller *The War between the Tates* (1974); but in many respects her
first novel is more revealing. Lurie knew intimately the world of the
university and its roles for women. Her father had been a professor
of sociology, and her mother had been a journalist before marrying
and giving up her career. At Radcliffe, Lurie had realized how completely male students dominated the campus. She had studied creative writing with Robert Hillyer, who told her class that they were
nice young ladies who could not write.[3] Patronized by many of her
lecturers, she nonetheless wrote an undergraduate dissertation on the
relation between the sexes in Jacobean comedy called "Love and
Money."

In her marriage to English professor Jonathan Bishop, Lurie strug-
gled to keep up her writing despite frequent rejection and twice gave
up writing altogether. At Amherst College, where the Bishops lived
from 1954 to 1957, she found the material for *Love and Friendship*,
which is dedicated to Jonathan Bishop, and also met the poet James
Merrill and his partner David Jackson, who became her close friends
and mentors. The Amherst English department had ten members
who socialized frequently, but Lurie was lonely. Bishop, "finding
himself at twenty-seven the sole support of four people, two of them
under the age of three, had become serious, distant, and preoccupied
with the need to finish his Ph.D. thesis and hold on to his job. He
left the house every weekday morning at 8.30 and returned at 5.30,
expecting dinner to be ready and the children quiet and out of the
way. In the evenings he read or corrected papers. He also usually
spent most of Saturday and Sunday at his office or in the library."
Such patterns were in accord with campus life. "Amherst in the
1950s," Lurie recalls,

was a patriarchal, family-centered society. Men went to work, and women stayed home and took care of the house and the children. There were no women on the faculty of Amherst College, and no women students. At faculty parties, the men tended to stand at one side of the room and talk shop, while the women sat at the other side, discussing domestic matters. (It occurs to me now that the reason the men stood up was that they sat down most of the day, reading and writing and having conferences. The women sat down because they had spent most of the day standing up, cooking and cleaning and washing and ironing and shopping and carrying babies and groceries.)[4]

Although its title suggests Jane Austen, *Love and Friendship* slyly updates George Eliot. The heroine and protagonist, Emily Stockwell Turner, is married to a Casaubon-like young English professor, Holman Turner, who teaches language and literature at Convers College in New England. Anxious about his career, Holman, like the other young faculty men in the English department, assists in the famous Humanities C course, directed by the ferocious Oswald McBane. It was "often called the theoretical (or the actual) center of education at Convers. All incoming freshmen were compelled to take it; more than that, all incoming instructors in the Languages and Literature Division were compelled to teach it. In many ways their individual futures at Convers depended on how well they did so, how quickly they caught on."[5]

McBane is Convers' version of Arthur Buchanan, and maybe every English department had such a totemic patriarch. As Allan Ingram writes to Francis Noyes (Lurie's surrogates for Merrill and Jackson), McBane is the "patent Great Old Man of Convers. Or Great Old Bear; he is far more bear than man. Think of him as that big gray grizzly up on his hind legs in the habitat group in the Natural History Museum. . . . McBane has just that profuse, dead-looking gray fur, heavy paws hanging down, fiercely quizzical expression." When his acolytes are slow to snap to, McBane retaliates, and "the merest slap from McBear's forepaw can knock the little animals off their perches" (76–77).

Teaching Hum C and attending the weekly meetings in which McBane pontificates about the lesson, is a sacred (and scared) obligation; "missing the weekly Hum C meeting was a sin forgiven only grudgingly even in the case of illness. Instructors often earned merit by attending when they should have been home in bed with severe colds" (29). Holman, a stoic and obedient scholar, never misses a meeting, but Emmy begins to suspect that Hum C worships false gods. She keeps trying to figure out the point of the assignments, but Holman condescends to her as Convers condescends to all women. "It would have been too disappointing," she thinks, "if there were no more of a mystery than this stupid word game at the heart of the mystery Convers" (23).

Bored and lonely, Emmy begins an affair with the seductive Will Thomas, a music teacher who is a bit like Eliot's Will Ladislaw. He is divorced from the beautiful and conventional Rosemary, now remarried to a successful doctor—more hints at *Middlemarch*. Their mutual friend Miranda, a witchy, wise, and unconventional faculty wife who engineers the affair between Emmy and Will, and who is a surrogate for Lurie herself, turns out to be really named Mary Ann.

Emmy comes from a rich family—indeed, her father is a trusteee of the college—and her private income allows the Turners to live in their own house in the country, rather than in the hideous "Huts," junior-faculty housing regularly inspected by Betsy Lumkin, whose husband is the dean in charge of faculty housing. These details are very accurate for the time. When I arrived at Princeton as a faculty wife in 1965, living in the high-rise barracks for junior faculty down by the lake, the houseplant tour of our apartments was the highlight of the social year, and the young faculty wives shared the expense of costly spices like saffron for our anxious entertaining of the department chair and his wife. Having seen academic culture first from the perspective of the beleaguered faculty wife, I always saw it double, even when I was a professor myself. The deans' wives presided over teas and other gatherings; in September 1970, when I got my Ph.D., a mischievous Princeton faculty friend wrote me a parody letter mocking the last vestiges of wifely decorum:

Dear Mrs. Showalter,

We were so pleased to receive your letter this morning. I am most gratified that the interest groups in contract bridge, needlecraft, and sewing have such appeal for you. I realize that belonging to all three will pose some scheduling troubles for you, but I sincerely hope that something can be worked out. We are especially eager for our very young junior faculty wives to maintain their interest in outside-the-home activities. Homemaking is such a full-time job, and you are right to want to develop new hobbies.

As for the personal part of your letter, I fully agree that recently the Princeton scene has been blighted by some fairly aggressive and unfeminine career girls who indulge in facile and annoying irony at the expenses of home makers and mothers like ourselves. With homemaking, church, and cooking for a family of growing children and a hardworking hungry husband (mine insists on a jello dessert every night!), we are not idlers but very busy people.

Cordially yours,

Mrs Grosvenor Morton-Townsend
Class of '35 and Dept of Hydraulics

In the end of the novel, Emmy stays with her husband and stays at Convers; although she has seen through the mystique of Hum C and the snobbery of the college, she gives her husband another chance, and even she, like John Aldridge, blames the Convers faculty wives for the worst gossip and pettiness of the place, seeing them as harpies, "swarming over the valley, with fat bodies and little sharp beaks" (301). In the terms of the novel, we have to assume that this is Emmy's destiny too—to become a Convers wife, a pourer of tea and guardian of the community values. The final scene shows the children playing a game with blindfolds—with the implication that refusing to see is the best and only practical solution. We know that Alison Lurie herself became a novelist and a professor of children's literature; we even know from her subsequent novel *Foreign Affairs* that life works out for Emmy. But the ending of *Love and Friendship*, typical of the fiction of the '60s, is wan and bleak.

Overall, feminism took a long time to seep into the academic novel, even when women were writing it. Carolyn Heilbrun started writing her academic mystery novels under the pseudonym Amanda Cross in 1963. Reading detective novels, especially those of Dorothy Sayers, had been a salvation for her "during a time of depression and some wild experimentation among the passions," and she wanted to contribute to the genre.[6] Why the pseudonym? First of all, Heilbrun felt that as an assistant professor of English at Columbia, she risked not getting tenure if it were known she wrote detective fiction. But she came to realize that that excuse was a smokescreen for something else: that as a young professional mother of three small children, she wanted a fantasy double, insouciant, rich, beautiful, single, parentless, a drinker, and a smoker. She created an alter ego, Professor Kate Fansler.

But the first Fansler novels, *In the Last Analysis* (1964) and *The James Joyce Murder* (1967), were clever puzzles with intellectual trimmings, very supportive of institutional and academic ideals. I didn't hear about them or read them then. Reading them now, I don't find Kate Fansler a model I'd want to emulate. She seems like a fantasy figure, with abstractly desirable qualities but no human depth and no lessons for someone in a real university. I'm especially struck by the way Kate Fansler rejects status in the academic community. The election plot of Snow and Baker seems to tempt Heilbrun, but she quickly moves outside of it. At a late stage in *The James Joyce Murder*, a retired woman professor approaches Kate with the offer of a college presidency, at the Jay College for Women. As Professor Knole explains, not too flatteringly, to be sure, "there's a shortage of really competent women around, let alone women who aren't married to men whose careers or egos foreclose any possibilities of their having a college president for a wife." Knole advises Kate to think about it carefully: "Remember, it's a position of power, and power is one of the most remarkable experiences there is." But Kate will have no truck with it; "I've never wanted power," she says.[7] We were still well short of a feminist heroine.

Two other '60s novels, Bernard Malamud's *A New Life* (1961) and Malcolm Bradbury's *Stepping Westward* (1965), are about writers encountering English departments in big state universities, where serious literature, James Joyce, and the rigors and theories of Hum C are much less important than Freshman Comp. Bernard Malamud had taught at Oregon State University for twelve years. He writes: "In 1949, when my son was two, we moved to Corvallis, Oregon, where I taught three days a week and wrote four." He had a sabbatical and a Rockefeller Grant, and spent 1956–57 in Italy.

I returned to Oregon to an improved situation after our year abroad. From a teacher of freshman grammar and technical report writing, I was transformed into a teacher of English literature, as though a new talent had been discovered in a surprised serf. What had happened was that the two gentlemen who administered the English department had heard I was getting a small reputation as a serious writer of fiction, and therefore I was no longer required to teach composition only, but might be allowed, even without a doctoral degree, to teach unsuspecting sophomores a little poetry, with even a touch of Shakespeare in the night. For this relief I gave happy thanks.[8]

But the novel is not about Malamud; when Philip Roth met Malamud at Oregon State University in 1961, he saw a man who looked like an insurance agent, "a conscientious, courteous, pinochle-playing workingman of the kind whose kibbutzing and conversation had been the background music of my childhood," a serious, reserved, unjoking man. *A New Life* is about S. Levin—Sy—who arrives in Marathon, Cascadia, in August 1950, to teach composition and to start anew. But, Roth observed, the real Malamud could not have been more unlike Sy Levin: "No more could Kafka have become a cockroach than Malamud could have metamorphosed into a Levin, comically outfoxed by an erotic mishap on the dark back roads of mountainous Oregon, and sneaking homewards, half-naked, at 3 A.M."[9]

That's a misleading account of the novel, which is pretty flat and much more concerned with the woes of teaching English in a service department than with erotic mishaps. The head of the English department at Cascadia College is Dr. Fairchild, author of *The Elements of Grammar*, the required text for all teachers. The students plagiarize, the faculty fish, the parents object to Hemingway on the syllabus, the coach gets his athletes passing grades. Levin protests that the comp course is "half dead . . . we ought to introduce some literature into the course so the students know that good writing means something more than good report writing" (248). This earnest request goes unheeded. Levin has some fantasies of writing scholarly articles, with titles like "The Forest as Battleground of the Spirit in Some American Novels," "Stranger as Fallen Angel in Western Fiction," and "The American Ideal as Self-Created Fiction"—vague and enormous topics at the opposite extreme from Jim Dixon's ship-building monograph, but reflecting the era's trendy obsessions. Levin isn't even especially exotic or Jewish, although he does miss New York.

The most interesting and subversive element of *A New Life* is Malamud's introduction of a character who would figure in later academic fiction: the wicked double in the form of the former faculty member whose office the new man inherits. In his case, it is Leo Duffy, "a disagreeable radical who made a lot of trouble" (35). Duffy smashed windows, failed more than half of his comp students, graded his papers late and let his dachshund pee on them, and ordered *The Communist Manifesto* from the college bookstore and "encouraged his students to discuss Marxism" (42). He seduced his students and prowled among the faculty wives. As Fairchild declares, every now and then "an evil genius will . . . raise his horns on a college campus" (46).

Malcolm Bradbury's novel has some of the same jokes and clichés about the provincial American university as Malamud's, but because Bradbury, and his hero James Walker, are coming from a depressed postwar England, even the crasser aspects of American Midwest campus life seem like a respite and a relief. Bradbury had been there himself:

> I was a new graduate, a young researcher and would-be novelist, going off to teach freshman composition and study American literature on a Midwestern American campus, at Indiana University. I belonged in fact to the Sabbatical Generation, the brand-new breed of scholars, students, critics, journalists, poets and novelists who used to gather on each side of the Atlantic every late summer to exchange themselves for their counterparts on the other, passing each other in midatlantic. A solemn, thesis-carrying generation . . . we went on Fulbrights, Hark-nesses, Commonwealth Funds, Jane Eliza Proctors, Henry Fellowships, the new huddled masses of the travel-grant age.

But he intended *Stepping Westward* to be "a fable of reversal— a semi-parodic rewriting of the older, familiar images of Anglo-American intercourse. . . . *Stepping Westward* was meant as a tale of a time when it was the turn of British and historical social innocence to meet American experience."[10]

The novel is set at Benedict Arnold University, in the town of Party in the "America heartland somewhere near the point where the various wests collide."[11] Like British provincial universities, Benedict Arnold is modeled on Olde England; the women's dorm is a version of Hampton Court, the Student Union is taken from Kings College Chapel, Cambridge, the campus bookstore is Anne Hathaway's cottage. Walker has been hired as a writer-in-residence to teach creative writing in the mistaken belief that he is an Angry Young Man, when in fact he is a stout, timid, repressed writer and part-time lecturer from Nottingham, with a nagging wife, a whiny daughter, and many bills. The university likes to have writers-in-residence around, and their traditional obligations are to write a novel in which the faculty appear only faintly disguised, resulting in "enormous publicity for the college" (14). Walker is thrilled to be lifted from his dull surroundings, to leave his wife and child behind for a year, and head to the land of anarchy and opportunity. So both sides are getting a good deal.

In the English Department at BA are the chairman, Harris Bourbon—"a big and totally unimpressive man who had been raised locally on a farm and had risen in the academic world through sheer endurance" (17)—and Bernard Froelich, the department Machiavelli and a kind of early version of the freewheeling, macho Jewish professor who would become the hero of academic fiction in the '70s. (Ironically, Sy Levin is far from being such an iconic figure.) Froelich is writing a book on "Plight" and hoping to cover all the bases. He is also "an ambitious man," a man who likes power and who hopes that Walker will be "a disintegrator and changer who will explode in faculty meetings and in the classrooms and somehow dislodge the world of dullness and fog . . . and so bring prestige to him and his causes" (315–16). Walker is no such person; but under Froelich's prodding he manages to create a scandal when he refuses to sign the university's loyalty oath. In the end, Walker leaves Party and gives up his fantasy of American anarchy; he goes back to Nottingham, sadder but wiser. Amusingly, this was the novel that got Bradbury a job as writer-in-residence at the University of California at Davis when I was stepping westward myself as a graduate student there in 1964–65, and I will always like it in part because we got to know Malcolm and his wife Elizabeth then.

The most elegiac of the academic novels of the '60s, the most melancholy and nostalgic for an era that was disappearing even faster than the author realized, was *The Department* (1968), by Gerald Warner Brace. Brace had a Ph.D. from Harvard and had taught English at Williams, Amherst, Dartmouth, Mount Holyoke, and Boston University. Like C. P. Snow, he admired Trollope above all the English novelists and wrote an introduction to *The Last Chronicle of Barset.* Reviewers inevitably compared him to Snow. One called *The Department* "an American equivalent" of *The Masters,* in its "witty and basically good-humored anatomy of every English Department there ever was."[12] But he must have deliberately closed his eyes to the pessimism, grief, and sense of failure in the book.

The narrator of *The Department* is Robert "Sandy" Sanderling, a professor of American literature with a degree from Harvard, who is planning his retirement speech: "I sleep well, mostly, but I compose farewell speeches," he begins. The retirement speech is a genre with its own requirements—"modest, unaffected, informal, witty, charming. . . . That's how professors are, that's their business." But Sandy has never felt that he belonged in the academic business, and writing his final remarks is a gloomy rite of passage in which he joins with his predecessors "for a time united in awareness of mortality. Each one sees himself standing for the last time in the light, saying the last words." Despite his discomfort with the academy, he can imagine no other life, and he thinks of retirement "as a sort of drifting off into darkness, with no return."[13]

Looking backward, he feels that he has accomplished very little. He is a not much of a scholar, "but under the rules of our game I must never seem to admit it" (15); his one novel, *Aftermath,* was not the book he hoped it would be; his marriage was a disaster; he has no real friends in his department. Moreover, the profession of teaching and the field of scholarship have changed and left him behind. "In the days of our youth, American literature was regarded with affection as a sort of family affair; it was full of nostalgia and pleasant local idiosyncracy—and all Bostonians had proprietary connections with it. . . . The sophisticated student was somewhat embarrassed about it, and in the days of my graduate study at Harvard, for example, no one in his right mind would think of 'doing work' in Melville, say, or even Hawthorne" (236). But now, "our departments are . . . full of very serious specialists whose first article of faith is that American literature embodies profundities and mysteries; . . . no amateur reader can be trusted with Mark Twain, for example; it takes a trained staff of authorities. Hawthorne is hardly suitable for undergraduate reading and is dealt with in the most advanced seminar" (237). The fashionable research topics of the day are phenomenology and death.

In many respects, *The Department* is an honorable and honest book, and yet, by 1968, it was as quaint as if it had been written in 1868, with the standard male faculty, unpleasant faculty wives, and wistful and yearning hero. There's really only one flash of what was actually going on in universities, and what was to come. In a seminar, Sandy encounters an early version of raised racial consciousness and militancy when he tries to illustrate the trickster figure by reading Brer Rabbit and the Tar Baby; his radical student Karsch tells him angrily, "Obviously Uncle Remus himself is an insult to all people with a social conscience" (248).

Sandy is a decent and well-meaning man, but he really doesn't have a clue what is happening in his profession. In the late 1960s, the Modern Language Association of America (MLA), the professional and scholarly association of professors of English and foreign literatures and languages, emerged from decades of respectable scholarly tedium to become a hotbed of radicalism. At the MLA's annual meeting in New York in 1968, a group of faculty were arrested protesting the organization's conservatism and old-boy governance. (I was working with their support group, answering phones in the hotel room.) Specifically and immediately they were demanding that the 1969 meeting, scheduled for Chicago, be canceled in retaliation for Mayor Daley's brutal treatment of anti–Vietnam War protestors the previous summer. But there was much more. Black studies had begun to challenge the whiteness of the profession and its reading lists. Feminists were beginning to organize to protest the status of women in the profession. The Stonewall riots had marked the beginnings of Gay Pride. And after many years of expansion, universities suddenly found themselves short of money, and the job market for new Ph.D.s in literature headed into a decline from which it has never recovered. In his MLA presidential address in 1969, the great Americanist scholar Henry Nash Smith borrowed the title of the

Dylan song to review the political upheavals in the profession: "Something Is Happening But You Don't Know What It Is, Do You, Mr. Jones?"[14]

But by that time, the wistful regrets of the merely well-intentioned Sanderlings were history. In a few more years, *The Department* would look like the ironic memoir of an unreliable narrator, the story of a extinct tribe, an academic *Remains of the Day*.

chapter 3

~

The Seventies

GLASS TOWERS

NOT UNTIL THE 1970S, when many writers were looking back on the previous decade with some bitterness and even rage at its excesses, did the academic novel begin to explore the political turmoil of the '60s. Even so, the impact of the women's movement is still muted. Feminism enters the university, but in indirect, unhappy, and hesitant ways. The university is no longer a sanctuary or a refuge; it is fully caught up in the churning community and the changing society; but it is a fragile institution rather than a fortress. That, at any rate, was how it looked in fiction, although for me personally it was an exhilarating decade. I had seen plenty of '60s excess and '70s aftermath on campus—caped sociology professors piping students into lecture-happenings on the recorder; religion professors holding love-ins during which we lay on waterbeds and watched porn films projected on the ceiling; English professors joining cults of many kinds; art professors holding a Black Mass in the chapel at which they sacrificed a sheep, much to the annoyance of the ag school. But I also saw the university opening up to real options of innovation in teaching and research.

The University of Watermouth, the imaginary campus of Malcolm Bradbury's *The History Man* (1975), epitomizes the new architecture and spaces that characterized the vision of the modern university. Modeled on the "plate-glass" universities such as Sussex and East Anglia that were built in the '60s and updated the redbricks, Watermouth is designed by the modernist Finnish architect Jop Kaakinen as "a futurist city," built on a hill, "a still expanding dream in white concrete, glass, and architectural free form." Watermouth, "having aspirations to relevancy, has made much of sociology," and a feature of the campus is the "high glass tower" of the Social Sciences Building. This glass house is the home of innovation, progress, imagination; but it is transparent and easily shattered, while at the center of the campus, the old patriarchal tower, "the high phallus, eolipilic in shape, of the boilerhouse chimney, the absolute focus, the point of maximum architectural eminence," will stand forever.[1]

In the novels of the '70s, glass becomes a mirror for the new academic self. As Kaakinen writes in his prospectus for Watermouth, "We are not alone making here the new buildings; we are creating too those new forms and spaces which are to be the new styles of human relationship. For an architecture is a society, and we are here making the society of the modern world of today" (47). Unlike the closes and snug chambers and paneled libraries of the Oxbridge style, the piazzas and student unions of the new university break down the barriers between men and women, town and gown, labor and learning, the body and the mind. But people who live in glass houses have no place to hide, and glass is also a weapon. Two novels published in 1970, the year I got my Ph.D., reflect this sense of ambivalence, uncertainty, and fear about academic change; both were by professors who eventually left the university themselves. Carolyn Heilbrun had been teaching at Columbia during the student protests of 1968, when Mark Rudd wrote in an open letter to President Grayson Kirk: "We will destroy your world, your corporation, your university." According to her friend Tom Driver, she was walking by Low Library when she saw that it was surrounded by police. On the steps of the library, faculty were lined up with armbands to act as buffers between the students inside and an expected police attack. "The next thing I knew I had on the armband and I was standing there," she wrote to Driver, who was in England.[2]

Is that radicalization or sleepwalking? Heilbrun's mixed emotions are reflected in the novel she wrote soon after, under her pseudonym Amanda Cross. In *Poetic Justice* (1970), the students have taken over the administration building, and the world has changed, in ways that Kate Fansler doesn't like and can barely begin to understand. Fansler describes herself, quoting W. H. Auden, as "unready to die, but already at the stage when one starts to dislike the young."[3] She loves the university, or at least the idea of a university, but seems as remote from her colleagues as from her students. When Frederick Clemance, the distant departmental god (based on Lionel Trilling) with whom she studied as a graduate student, actually deigns to invite her to sit in on a thesis defense, Kate thinks that so "Frederick the Great might have spoken to one of his courtiers" (13). These Buchanans and McBanes, the lords of the department, were getting a little tedious by 1970. Yet rather than laughing at him, Fansler herself acts like a haughty Kate the Great, who parodies the curriculum reforms in the English department as having to hire someone who speaks Swahili, or, most unrealistically, teach a seminar on the novels of Bulwer-Lytton. Indeed, Fansler seems like a female version of Clemance in many of her attitudes.

Toward the end of the novel, however, Heilbrun introduces a counterself to Fansler. Emilia Airhart teaches drama and writes off-Broadway plays "so very with it that no one in the whole Department realized for years that Emilia was writing them" (64), just as Heilbrun had delighted in writing detective novels under a pseudonym. Moreover, while Kate Fansler is elegant, slender, patrician, and given to an intellectual form of Nora Charles banter, Emilia Airhart is "a large woman with flat shoes, wide skirts, and glasses" (64). Kate is married but childless and spends a lot of time gossiping about the department; Emilia has five children and never "has anything to do with anything in the Department" (64). Finally, while Kate is deferential to and intimidated by Clemance, Emilia thinks he is "pompous, a company man, and a male chauvinist" (64). All in all, she sounds a lot more lively and interesting than Kate Fansler; like her namesake, Emilia is a female pioneer, whose experiences and views are much closer to Heilbrun's personal politics than student sit-ins. And indeed her appearance and family situation are also more like Heilbrun's than are Fansler's. Nonetheless, Emilia too is sniffy about feminism. "There is now even an organization for liberating women —utter nonsense. Women are liberated the moment they stop caring what other women think of them" (106).

Similarly, Kate isn't sure whether she sides with the revolution. True, she sides with the radical group that wants to bring in adult education (i.e., working-class men and older women); yet at the end of the novel, she is hopelessly awash in emotion about the ancient university and its towers of privilege: "Kate, walking in the dusk toward the subway, was again visited by this sense of—what did one call it, affection, love, devotion?—and again wondered: toward what do I feel this sense of loyalty, a quite out-of-date emotion? . . . Suffice it perhaps to say that here was an institution for which she would willingly work; the University was not, for her, simply a place to pursue a career" (163). It would be another ten years before Heilbrun could see the university as a glass house.

The careerism that Kate Fansler deplores got its comeuppance as well in *Deadly Meeting* (1970), by Robert Bernard, the pseudonym of Robert B. Martin, a professor of Victorian literature at Princeton, who retired to England in 1975 and began a second career as a mystery writer.[4] The genre seems to have attracted an unusual number of English professors, whereas people who regard themselves primarily as authors tend to write mainstream novels, with Trollopean plots, character studies, or social analysis. On the superficial level, genre fiction probably appeals to the "I can do that" feeling many critics get after studying literary texts in minute detail: minor genres have easy-to-follow rules, and everyone understands that the author is only playing a game. Mysteries also offer some deeper satisfactions, however; they combine well with satire, and it is more fun to portray your enemy being whacked, or stooping to murder, than to try to write an empathetic life story that also conveys your animosity. The genre also lends itself to exploring small, closed societies, with intense passions lavished on matters that seem trivial to outsiders, long-standing grudges and debts, and almost-forgotten secrets from the past.

The "deadly meeting" in Bernard's title is the annual convention of the MLA. But Bernard's novel is an anomaly, for by the time of its publication, the MLA had been torn by radical protest. In the 1970s, a shrinking job market and cutbacks in the booming budgets of the previous decade gave the convention a quality of tension and desperation, of haves and have-nots locked in Darwinian struggle, which it has never lost. It was already on its way to becoming a staple of the academic novel, legendary for its size (about 12,000 people attend), for its promiscuity both intellectual and sexual, for its energy, its anarchy, and its absurdity.

But not a trace of these cataclysms is reflected in Bernard's novel, in which the placid male community of Wilton College (probably Princeton again, *hélas*) is still blind to women, unaware of race, virulently homophobic, and openly anti-Semitic. Considering that R. B. Martin himself was homosexual and a sophisticated man who later made a happy cosmopolitan life for himself in London, reading *Deadly Meeting* is in retrospect like opening a dark closet stuffed with masquerade, hypocrisy, and denial. The mystery genre may have offered Martin, like many other English professors, an oblique way to address the mysteries and secrets of the academy.

The narrative center of the novel is Bill Stratton, a decent, hard-working English professor with a private income, happy marriage, and no children, who is the focus for the story of the murder of the department chair, Peter Jackson, at the MLA. Bill and his wife Carrie have a domestic life that resembles a mix of Bogart and Bacall in '40s films—lots of wisecracks, lots of sexy gestures—with erudite literary allusions. Other women in the novel fare less well than Carrie—the usual stupid faculty wives, this time with "matronly breasts," or "improbably tilted breasts"; a "hard, driving, and arrogant" woman graduate student named Susan Englander with a "breathtaking body," who is widely hated despite being one of the most intelligent students in the department ever; and a nutty old medievalist from England, Dame Millicent Hetheredge, who trains dogs in her spare time and also writes mystery novels under the name "Deirdre Desiree." If I had been able to read this novel in 1966, when I first came to Princeton as a faculty wife trying to finish a dissertation on Victorian women writers, I would have been wiser than to have approached Martin for some scholarly support and advice. I still wince at the memory of his polite brush-off.

The MLA is held at "Devonport," a fictional setting that sounds like Atlantic City. In some respects this academic gathering is recognizable; Bernard may have been the first academic to describe the star system in literary studies: "Nowadays the men who read papers at the meetings tended to be either super-stars of the professions who drew audiences of a thousand or more, or earnest young men in a hurry who hoped for offers of better jobs elsewhere once they had read a paper at M.L.A." But in other respects it seems like a nineteenth-century world, as the references to men suggest. Although, by 1970, there were many women at the MLA, including me, Stratton sees only "large men in sober suits with large, sober faces" and nuns: "Every Catholic women's college in the country must have sent a major portion of its faculty." The only other female presence at this MLA is the pretty young editorial assistant Stratton and his chums meet at a publishers' party, one of the many "Smith and Radcliffe graduates who drifted into publishing every spring."

The murder victim, Peter Jackson, is cruel, overbearing, bigoted, philandering, and—worst of all—a critical barbarian. At the convention, he does not recognize Stratton's rhetorical question—"What porridge had John Keats?"—as a quotation from Browning and an ironic comment on those yahoos who would reduce great poetry to mundane factual detail. Moreover, Jackson thinks it would be amusing to do some research on nineteenth-century porridge consumption in Hampstead and write a little piece about it for *Notes and Queries*. A decade later such interests would become the basis of cultural studies, but in 1970, it marks Jackson as a philistine, and we know at once that he has to die. After Peter has been poisoned, poor Bill becomes department chairman and discovers that Jackson has been keeping blackmail files on the senior faculty, including one unlucky fellow's arrest for picking up an undercover policeman in a bar. Killing off Peter Jackson and being revenged on bullying homophobic men offers Martin some literary satisfaction, but there remains an underlying nostalgia for the university as a men's club despite its pressures.

Women writing about the MLA in the 1970s inhabited a parallel universe, one in which women were visible, at least to each other, and they cast a cold eye on the agonistic rituals of their male colleagues and their worship of the canon. Joyce Carol Oates, who was teaching at the University of Windsor in the early '70s, took the perspective of the woman writer who is the subject of a nonsuperstar panel. In her story "Angst," published in *The Hungry Ghosts* (1974), novelist Bernadine Donovan slips anonymously into a session on her work at the Palmer House in Chicago. Her panel is in the Cameo Room, while down the hall, in the Grand Ballroom, three big-deal male critics are discussing "Black Humor and Psychosis."[5] Of course, all the losers, nobodies, and weirdly named women provincials invisible to Robert Martin—Jolene Snyder from Milwaukee Community College, Bobbie Rae Dean of Lamar Tech—are going to her session, while the well-dressed and hung-over young men from Princeton and Columbia are heading briskly to the ballroom. Only one of the panelists is male—"a thin, downlooking young man . . . from a small community college in New Rochelle" (196). And the papers, pedantic and paranoid, mumbled or shouted, either attribute Donovan's work to her influences—Woolf, Proust, Swift—or find hidden messages behind her themes. As Donovan fights back tears, a red-haired madwoman gets up, declaring that she is Bernadine Donovan and has be dragged away. Here, as in other stories in the collection, Oates explained, she "wanted to illustrate from the inside . . . how ambition, lust for fame and prestige, and egotism, can ruin the lives of presumably intelligent people."[6]

But what was it like for those provincial women, patronized even by other women professionals, in academic life in the 1970s? In Gail Godwin's *The Odd Woman* (1974), Jane Clifford attends the MLA conference in New York, when she is a graduate student looking for a job. She is staying at the Americana Hotel, sharing a room with another female graduate student, an Indian specialist in Renaissance poetry named Deiri. For Jane and Deiri, the convention is a disheartening series of awkward, insulting, and dismissive interviews. One department chairman tells Jane that she reminds him of "a fascinating woman who was formerly in his department. She went mad."[7] At least Jane meets Gabriel Weeks, a married man who becomes her lover, when she attends his paper on the Pre-Raphaelites. She even has a flash of a new kind of pulp romance genre: "In which the heroine always met her man at the MLA—everybody seemed to be doing it these days" (76). If pulp romances offered the puzzle-solving challenge of well-written mysteries, the genre would probably exist. Unfortunately, most heroines meet their man not at the MLA but in the classroom, and the genre had morphed into the sexual harassment saga by the 1990s.

Godwin had taught at the Universities of Iowa and Illinois, and Jane Clifford is an English professor who teaches Romantic and Victorian literature at a university in the Midwest, in a town "like a disturbing dream," in a "dead-flat prairie" (24). Jane's "profession was words and she believed in them deeply" (3). In her introduction to a recent British edition of the novel, Nicci Gerrard emphasizes Jane's addiction to the plots of the Victorian novels she studies: "She

continually reads and re-reads and edits herself to discover her disso-
nances and her textual glitches."[8] Jane sees herself as a character-type
in a story, "career woman" or "spinster" or "professor of English" or
"intellectual" or "Romantic" or "lady pedant." In particular, she compares herself to a heroine by George Eliot, on whom she has written
her dissertation. "If George Eliot were making me a heroine in one
of her books," Jane thinks, "though I doubt my character would
meet her standards for a heroine—what would she say in that long,
involved, philosophic passage where she justifies who and what I am
and how I got that way?" (22).

I had also written part of my dissertation on George Eliot and had
taught English in a flat prairie town, and I was thrilled to discover
Jane Clifford, who was almost exactly my own age in 1974, and a
recognizable double. The American critic Rachel Brownstein locates
The Odd Woman in the contexts of the women's movement and feminist criticism and believes "it is hard not to read the novel today
as an expression of the feminism of the seventies." During this decade, Brownstein argues, "real and fictional literary women like Jane
Clifford were fascinating to themselves and others as never before—
or perhaps since. . . . A conspicuous literary legacy of the women's
movement in the second half of the twentieth century is fiction
about English majors by English majors, who set about deliberately
to revise the standard heroine's character and life story." Not only
women writers but women professors "seemed attractive role models,
professional women who thought professionally about love and its
images and stories, achieving, as they did so, an enviable integration
of love and work."[9]

Certainly *The Odd Woman* is one of the few academic novels in
which professors actually seem to work; Jane's bed light even has four
intensities—night, work, television, and read. Much of the novel
involves her insomniac lecture preparation for the section of a course
on "Women in Literature" that she team-teaches with her friend
Sonia Marks, a charismatic lecturer who believes that "good teaching
is one-fourth preparation and three-fourths theatre" (49). Sonia has
everything Jane wants—tenure, a husband, children, a book from
Oxford University Press—but Jane has decided to start the course
with Gissing's *The Odd Women* because of its "unrelenting pessimism. It was one of the few nineteenth-century novels she could

think of in which every main female character who was allowed to live through the last page had to do so alone" (27). For similar reasons, I too taught Gissing in the 1970s and 1980s. Jane also struggles to grade the papers of her three favorite students, the black scholarship girl, Portia; the motorcycle hippie, Howard; the angel genius, Sheldon. Some of the most compelling passages in the book, for me, are those in which Jane tries to decide how to evaluate these very different kinds of student writers.

In contrast to male authors of academic novels, Gail Godwin is also a helpful and candid guide to academic secrets and mysteries. In Carlos Baker's *A Friend in Power*, for example, Ed Tyler knows in advance that he is going to get a Guggenheim fellowship but doesn't explain how. In *The Party at Cranton*, Waithe hints that sucking up to Arthur Buchanan is the route to Guggenheim success. In *The Odd Woman*, though, Sonia Marks tells Jane that when you are on the list, you get a letter a month early, asking you for a budget. "And that means you've got it and have time to tell your chairman and everything, but everyone's afraid to say anything until it's really announced" (412). That piece of inside information spared me another humiliating conversation with my male colleagues, who all somehow knew this already.

But when it comes to love, Jane Clifford's life is more fantasy than fulfillment. As a narrator, Jane deserves credit for the range and frankness of her sexual imaginings: sex with students, with pilots, and even with the Enema Bandit, a sexual pervert attacking women in the university. One night she stays up drawing a series of lurid pornographic murals. In real life, she has experienced no more than "fourteen furtive fucks" with Gabriel Weeks over a period of two years (398). Jane is conflicted not only emotionally but also intellectually. She thinks she believes in the sanctity of the canon, in Matthew Arnold's dictum that literature is the best that has been thought and said and that we study it for those reasons. She thinks that she is a psychological realist and a moralist, like George Eliot and the Victorians. But at the same time she is disturbed by the contradictions in her own personality, beginning to question the unitary "self" and to think through the issues of identity and wholeness that were being raised in poststructuralism in the mid-1970s. "Sometimes, lately, she wondered if the concept of the 'self' was a myth which had died with the nineteenth century" (21). These contradictions make Jane a member of my personal pantheon of inspiring female academics in fiction. As Gerrard says, Jane "may wind the clock, check timetables, arrive at airports with hours to spare, pack her case meticulously, think ahead and look behind, hold in her head the barren day; she may be anxious and decorous," yet she "is honestly and honourably trying to find her individual truth . . . in spite of her own fears."[10]

Malcolm Bradbury's *The History Man* (1975) is the harshest indictment of the academic and personal transformations of the '70s. It takes place from October 2 to December 15, 1972, at the University of Watermouth, a new campus set in a city like Brighton. In an Author's Note (a typical device of the British university novel), Bradbury disclaims any relation to academic reality: "Not only does the University of Watermouth, which appears here, have no relation to the real University of Watermouth (which does not exist) or to any other university; the year 1972, which also appears, bears no relation to the real 1972, which was a fiction anyway; and so on."

But the personalities, actions, and environments of Watermouth are recognizable emblems of the nastiest sides of late '60s and early '70s feminism, hipness, leftism, and sexual liberation. Watermouth, with its halls called Hobbes, Kant, Marx, Hegel, Toynbee, and Spengler, is the very model of the cutting-edge new university; the campus is "one of those dominant modern environments of multifunctionality that modern man creates: close it down as a university, a prospect that seemed to become increasingly possible as the students came to hate the world, and the world the university, and you could open it again as a factory, a prison, a shopping precinct."[11] Some spirit of tolerance remains, as students produce a Marxist version of *King Lear*, or a capitalist version of Brecht; there is student life, with the Women's Lib Nude Encounter Group, the Revolutionary Student Alliance, and the Gaysoc Elizabethan Madrigal Evening (shades of *Lucky Jim*); but the bedraggled students look like "the winter retreat of Napoleon's army from Moscow" (65), and the utopian dream of the '60s university has been eaten away by locusts. "In the rain the buildings are black; the concrete has stained; the glass grown dirty; the services diminished. The graffiti experts have been at work . . . there has been a small fire in the library; rapes and

muggings occur occasionally in the darker corners of this good society" (66). The remnants of old Watermouth, the traditional city and
its people, are being demolished by the machines of the modern city.
Bradbury himself admitted a few years later that he was "depressed
the whole time I was writing *The History Man*. It's certainly my
bleakest book."[12]

Presiding over this fallen world is the demonic figure of Professor
Howard Kirk, the "history man." Kirk is actually a radical sociologist and a media don; he is a community activist, "a terror to the
selfish bourgeoisie," a "theoretician of sociability," and the author of
"two well-known and disturbing books" (3), artfully unstructured,
like his parties and his seminars. Teaching at Watermouth is edgy:
"You never know quite what to expect. There are classes where you
have, on arrival, to eat something, or touch each other, or recount
last night's dreams, or undress. . . . There are others where you have
to sit and listen to tutors in self-therapy," and those in which the
students become "objects of therapy, problem-bearers, and where
an apparently casual remark . . . will lead to a sudden, psychic foray
from a teacher who will dive down in to your unconscious with three
shrewd enquiries and come up clutching something in you called
'bourgeois materialism' or 'racism.' Howard's classes are especially
famous for being punitive in this way" (128).

With his Zapata mustache and "hairy loose waistcoats" (5),
Howard is a desirable figure who teaches a famous course in revolu-
tions; sleeps with his women students and his better-looking female
colleagues; bullies his male students, especially if they have different
political views; and ceaselessly schemes to keep the campus in an
uproar. He is the Machiavellian product of a new era in which people transcend history and make their own identities, just as he has
reinvented himself.

Barbara Kirk is Howard's wife, partner, and ally: "At this minute
just a person, as she puts it, trapped in the role of wife and mother,
in the limited role of woman in our society; but of course she, too,
is a radical person and quite as active as Howard in her way" (3). But
his version of history and change does not work as well for her, and
Bradbury uses her story as a counterpoint to Howard's empower-
ment. As he told John Haffenden, "Barbara is in a sense the hidden central character of the whole novel. If it's a tragedy, the tragic

heroine is Barbara. But the point is that her story is not fully represented until you think about it when you've put the book down—and then it's possible to discern what it might have been."[13]

Bradbury traces the marriage of the Kirks as a symbol of history itself. They begin as '50s working-class scholarship students, but they are transformed by the '60s. Their marriage conceals a lot of competition and antagonism, and in some respects the novel is a British "War between the Kirks," a parallel to Alison Lurie's *War between the Tates*, published the same year, about the covert battles between academic men and their wives. First, Barbara has a baby, trumps him because she has "published in the ultimate way" (30). Then Howard begins to feel that she is "out to destroy him." They had moved, in sociological terms, from a consensus model of marriage to a conflict model, "in which interests were starkly defined, and ultimate resolution must depend on violence or the defeat of one of the parties" (31). Howard fights back by writing a book about the restructuring of sexual roles in Britain, which Barbara thinks is about them and a "smart punishment for the baby" (33).

In 1968, the Kirks' lives seem to merge with the zeitgeist. "Everything seemed wide open; individual expectations coincided with historical drive" (48). Not even Watermouth seems radical enough for Howard: "Nothing *was* radical enough for the Kirks that year. Howard stared at the campus from the sit-in and what he said was: 'I think this is a place I can work against'" (49). Nothing since has equaled the "intimacy, warmth, and consensus" of that magical year (50). The Kirks feel that they are "somehow still on the fulcrum between end and beginning, in a history where an old reality is going and a new one coming, living in a mixture of radiance and radical indignation, burning with sudden fondnesses, raging with sudden hates, waiting for a plot, the plot of historical inevitability, to come" (51). Howard is writing a new book called *The Defeat of Privacy*, which is about "the fact that there are no more private selves, no more private corners in society, no more private properties, no more private acts. . . . There are no concealments any longer, no mysterious dark places of the soul" (73).

Barbara's story is that of the faculty wife at the moment when she was becoming desperate, when her species was becoming extinct, when the women's movement had cut her off from the pleasures of her role without giving her a new one. She is the one who has to do the work behind Howard's glamorously spontaneous life. When they plan their annual start-of-year party, Barbara is unenthusiastic: "Maybe I'm getting old . . . all I see in my mind are dirty glasses" (8). From the beginning of the novel, she sees Howard as a master of exploitation, chiefly of herself. And she is haunted by suicide. As she and Howard are shopping for their party, she tells him about a boy who came to one of their parties who has killed himself: "He thought life was silly" (15). Howard is uninterested, but Barbara sees its as significant: "Doesn't it worry you at all that so many of our friends feel that way now? do things like that now? That they seem tired and desperate? Is it our ages? Is it that the political excitement's gone?" (16). Barbara is one of the many Emma Bovary figures in academic fiction. She has a lover, a young actor named Leon, whom she meets for weekends in London that include shopping sprees at Biba, the height of early '70s fashion. But Leon tells her that he is going off for five months for an Australian tour of *Much Ado about Nothing*, and Barbara sinks into a depression that reaches its climax in the second of two epic parties given by the Kirks, which frame the book.

At the first party, the Kirks' old friend Henry Beamish, left behind by his profession and scorned by his wife, smashes a bedroom window and slashes his arm "savagely on the glass," requiring twenty-seven stitches. Howard does not want to accept this gesture as a suicide attempt, but his lover, Flora Beniform, a voice of wisdom in the novel, sees it as "an act of anger and despair. . . . Suicide is the traditional way of nullifying oneself as an actor" (117). Flora rescues Henry, although everyone else at the party is making too much noise to notice. But at the second, the end-of-term party, Barbara, in a new silvery dress, smashes a window and slices her arm on the broken glass. This time no one hears; for "as always at the Kirks' parties . . . all the people are fully occupied" (230). By Bradbury's standards, a hustler like Howard Kirk can only be a villain, can only smash and destroy people, institutions, and values.

After Malcolm Bradbury's death in 2000, David Lodge wrote in an obituary that "he was my literary twin."[14] They had been friends and colleagues at the University of Birmingham: but while Bradbury utterly deplored the movers and shakers, the sexist rogues and academic climbers of the new universities, Lodge rather enjoyed them.

No less a moralist than Bradbury, with whom he shared the experience of postwar education, and a serious and committed Catholic to boot, Lodge saw the heady optimism, sexual charge, and educational energy of the '60s and reveled in their capacities to break down barriers and engender boisterous laughter.

The genesis of his novel *Changing Places* (1975) came when he took a leave of absence from the University of Birmingham in January 1969 to

> take up the post of visiting associate professor at the University of California, Berkeley. At that time, both campuses, like most campuses, were in the throes of the student revolution; but whereas Birmingham's "occupation" had been a relatively mild-mannered and good-humoured affair, in Berkeley there was something like civil war in progress, with police chasing demonstrators through the streets with shotguns and clouds of teargas drifting across the campus. And if Birmingham was timidly responding to the vibrations emanating from Swinging London, Berkeley was at the leading edge of the Permissive Society, the Counter-Culture, Flower Power and all the rest of the 1960s baggage.[15]

But while Bradbury saw permissiveness, collectivity, swinging, protest, and the counterculture as sinister, and the Howard Kirks who exploited it as monsters, Lodge identified with the other side, let its comic potential flourish openly, rather than surreptitiously (for Howard Kirk is so very deliciously awful, seductive, and power-mad as to be quite attractive). Although *Changing Places* is critical of the excesses, pretensions, and posturings of the '60s university, overall it affirms the carnivalesque and liberatory aspects of the decade without sourness or cynicism. As Lodge said in an interview, "I don't think that in good faith I could satirize in a destructive way an institution which I belong to. I think I can stand back from the academic profession enough to see its absurd and ridiculous aspects, but I don't think it's really wicked or mischievous."[16]

Lodge himself was an experienced novelist, a critic, and literary theorist of distinction, and *Changing Places* reflects his fascination with narrative theory and its binaries. *Changing Places* begins with a sentence that has by now become famous: "High, high above the

North Pole, on the first day of 1969, two professors of English Literature approached each other at a combined velocity of 1200 miles per
hour."[17] On one Boeing 707 is Philip Swallow from the University
of Rummidge; on the other, Morris Zapp from the State University
of Euphoria. They are undertaking a six-month exchange, a device
Lodge uses along with several other binaries, to talk about higher
education, England and America, and the state of the novel. Zapp
and Swallow trade offices, jobs, and even wives; and both are liberated by the experience.

Rummidge—Zapp's wife hears it as "Rubbish"—is a dim version
of Birmingham; Euphoric State is a heightened version of Berkeley.
They share a singular architectural feature—"a replica of the leaning
Tower of Pisa, built of white stone and twice the original size at
Euphoric State, and of red brick and to scale at Rummidge" (8). Similarly, Swallow and Zapp epitomize their respective academic cultures. Swallow is "a man with a genuine love of literature" but an
inability to settle on a field (11). He is a survivor of the British exam-
ination system, a man who excels at taking exams and at giving
them, and his ideal critical work would be "a concise, comprehensive
survey of English literature consisting entirely of questions" (13)—a
kind of Times Literary Supplement literary quiz. He teaches much
and publishes little and is unhappy with his marriage and sex life and
life maintenance routines.

Morris Zapp, the American, is one of academic fiction's most
hilarious and revolutionary characters—an academic who approaches
the university as if it were a corporation, aims for financial and sexual success, loves power, and is not despised or punished for being
crass, sexist, competitive, hedonistic, and horny. As Lodge has en-
dearingly said, "There's a little bit of Morris Zapp in me, I think,
and I respond to that witty, abrasive, thrusting Jewish type of American academic: I always feel that life starts to move twice as fast when
you're in their company."[18] My only reservation about Morris Zapp
is that I can't imagine his female equivalent; a woman professor this
tough, feisty, and confident would have to be bumped off.

Zapp, Lodge writes, is the product of the American system of
higher education in which the surviving Ph.D. candidate has been so
tested and tormented that he is "well-primed to enter a profession as
steeped in the spirit of free enterprise as Wall Street, in which each

scholar-teacher makes an individual contract with his employer, and is free to sell his services to the highest bidder" (10). Indeed, Zapp is a natural player—to use the term academic hotshots in the United States reserve for the inner circle—but I disagree with Lodge that he is typical of American Ph.D.s, who often take their values from Oxbridge. Zapp is precocious: "Zapp was the man who had published articles in *PMLA* while still in graduate school; who, enviably offered his first job by Euphoria State, had stuck out for twice the going salary, and got it; who had published five fiendishly clever books (four of them on Jane Austen) by the time he was 30 and achieved the rank of full professor at the same precocious age" (15). Zapp has "the professional killer instinct" (10); he aims to be the highest paid professor of English in the world, and his ideal critical work would be "a series of commentaries on Jane Austen which would work through the whole canon, one novel at a time, saying absolutely everything that could possibly be said about them," from every critical angle, with the purpose of shutting up every other Austen critic forever.

In his "Faustian moments," Zapp dreams of "going on, after fixing Jane Austen, to do the same job on the other major English novelists . . . spreading dismay through the whole industry, rendering scores of his colleagues redundant: periodicals would fall silent, famous English departments be left deserted like ghost towns" (35). I find that ambition one of the funniest passages in the book, and Zapp's longing to wipe out the academy and be the only professor left standing—he later realizes that this is an impossible dream—is one of his most charmingly boyish qualities.

Meanwhile, Zapp has hit a plateau and, at the age of forty, can't decide where to go next. He understands that innovation is unlikely to come from elite institutions and that Rummidge is a perfect venue for a man of his gifts and ambititon: "Rummidge wasn't the greatest university in the world, agreed, but the set-up was wide open to a man with energy and ideas. Few American professors wielded the absolute power of a Head of Department at Rummidge. Once in the driver's seat, you could do whatever you liked. With his expertise, energy, and international contacts, he could really put Rummidge on the map, and that would be kind of fun" (212).

While professors gossip that many characters in academic novels are based on real people, Morris Zapp and Stanley Fish are the only acknowledged doubles. In a profile of Fish for the *New Yorker*—Zapp would have loved it!—Larissa MacFarquhar noted that

> at a fairly early point in his career, Fish and his love of shopping were immortalized, by the novelist David Lodge, in a comic fictional character named Morris Zapp. . . . Morris Zapp only added lustre and comic depth to Stanley Fish, and Fish himself was thrilled. "Stanley rather exaggerates the resemblance, actually," Lodge says. Morris Zapp made his first appearance in 1975, in *Changing Places*, an academic satire. Morris Zapp, Lodge wrote, "was that rarity among American Humanities Professors, a totally un-alienated man. He liked America. . . . His needs were simple: a temperate climate, a good library, plenty of inviting ass around the place and enough money to keep him in cigars and liquor and to run a comfortable modern house and two cars."

Explaining his fascination with Fish, Lodge comments, "Stanley was a very glamorous figure to me. He had an Alfa Romeo. He had an unashamed love of popular culture at a time when most academics would only indulge that covertly—it was thought to be slightly unprofessional. He loved pop music; he used to write his books while watching baseball on television; and he was completely un-awed by European culture. He had these witticisms like 'Travel narrows the mind.'"

MacFarquhar wonders whether the fictional character has actually influenced the man:

> Could it be that, in some strange way, Morris Zapp is exacting a Dorian Gray price for all the fat years? Oddly, although Lodge didn't intend Zapp to be an accurate portrait of Fish, and certainly didn't intend him as a prediction, Fish's life has, in number of ways, taken a Zappian course. Zapp's marriage broke up, and then, some years later, Fish got a divorce. Zapp was, underneath it all, a rather melancholy character. At the age of forty, he had already begun to brood about the meaning of life. Morris Zapp, Lodge wrote, "could think of nothing he wanted to achieve that he hadn't achieved already, and this depressed him. . . . He could only significantly increase his salary either

by moving to some god-awful place in Texas or the Mid-West . . . or by switching to administration." When Lodge wrote these sentences, Fish seemed to suffer no such affliction. He was, in a sense, more Morris Zapp than Morris Zapp. Not anymore. "He's certainly not as abrasive and aggressive as he used to be, " Lodge says. "He's more gentle and qualified and a little world-weary. He says, 'I keep saying the same thing and getting misunderstood in the same way.' Fish has always played up the Stanley Fish act, to outrage people or make them laugh, but whereas in years past this joyful routine just added a little extra zing to his regular personality, like a big gold medallion or elevator shoes, these days he seems to be playing Stanley Fish like a part he has memorized. Although he is more famous and better paid than ever, and although his books, still widely read and still witty, stand as monuments in their fields, something about the performance seems to have gone stale for him. Getting audiences to hate him isn't as fun as it used to be."[19]

Even Fish's publicity plays on the Zapp connection. In a press release from Harvard University Press at the end of 2000 accompanying the galleys of Fish's book on Milton, his editor, Lindsay Waters, wrote: "Everyone knows that Stanley Fish is the character Morris Zapp in David Lodge's best-selling novel *Changing Places*. Professor Zapp, the anti-hero of that novel, is said to be working on his magnum opus, a comprehensive account of the work of one of the greatest writers in the language. This book on Milton is that book we have been waiting for."

Finally Zapp/Fish was one of the great lusty Jewish characters in the academic novel, a brother in some ways to Philip Roth's professorial alter egos. Toward the end of the '70s, Roth published two quasi-academic novels, *The Professor of Desire* (1977) and *The Ghost Writer* (1979), using the campus setting and faculty figures to explore questions of Jewish literary identity. David Kepesh is the hero of *The Professor of Desire*.[20] As the title suggests, Kepesh connects his profession as a teacher of comparative literature with his secret sexual longings; this combination of literature and lust, particularly characteristic of Roth, would soon be taboo, but even in the late '70s it is shocking. Kepesh is tormented by his broken marriage to Helen, childless, and convinced he can never be happy with only one woman.

He is also obsessed with the great European writers of disillusion and despair; Chekhov, Kafka, Mann, Doestoevsky, Tolstoy, and Flaubert. On a holiday in Prague, Kepesh dreams of meeting Kafka's whore—a moment that brings sex and suffering together. As in *The Ghost Writer*, where Nathan Zuckerman fantasizes that he is going to marry Anne Frank, the image violates and eroticizes a sacred Jewish icon. For Kepesh, heroism is to face reality, however scandalous and forbidden, without illusions and with utter honesty. As another doppelganger, the concentration camp survivor Barbatnik, tells Kepesh the vision that kept him alive was to become "a human being, someone that could see and understand how we lived, and what was real, and not to flatter myself with lies" (257).

The Ghost Writer is one of Roth's masterpieces, the first in his trilogy of novels about another surrogate writer-figure, Nathan Zuckerman.[21] Set at Athene College, it features Zuckerman's effort to become the protégé and spiritual son of the writer E. I. Lonoff, a version of Bernard Malamud. Zuckerman is asking questions about Jewish identity and narrative: "The difficulties of telling a Jewish story—How should it be told? In what tone? To whom should it be told? To what end? Should it be told at all?—was finally to become *The Ghost Writer*'s theme. But before it became a theme, it apparently had to be an ordeal."[22]

Both Kepesh and Zuckerman take the academic novel into another dimension, beyond satire, into a world where the literary, the scholarly, the postmodern, and the political converge. In Roth, the academic novel merges with the Jewish novel, both concerned with distinctive subcultures in America; but academe started as a place of privilege, inhabited by an elite who knew they belonged, whereas the central characters in Jewish novels were outsiders, troubled by dual identities and divided loyalties. Along with Zapp, Kepesh and Zuckerman reflect a real change in American universities: by the end of the 1970s, even bastions of WASP tradition like Princeton had many Jewish professors, and anti-Semitism was universally deplored. In the 1980s and afterward, some of the best American novelists used the university as a setting and centered fictions on the Jewish professor, who spoke for a dark, even terrifyingly apocalyptic, vision. But while Kepesh and Zuckerman found a place in the academy, and Zapp rose to stardom, their female counterparts were still struggling.

chapter 4

❧

The Eighties

FEMINIST TOWERS

L ITERARY THEORY AND women's studies became institutional-
ized in the university at almost the same time in the 1980s.
Theory was the ticket to intellectual and professional legiti-
macy, and it became the basis of the academic star system, in which
universities hotly competed for the services of a few celebrated, expensive, and mobile theorists, while anonymous exploited masses
taught literature and composition. But the '80s were also the decade
of feminist literary criticism and theory and the moment when
women appear in the academic novel as serious contenders for tenure, status, and all the glittering prizes.

But, at least when women are writing the books, these newly
empowered female academics are oddly ambivalent about status, tormented by power, and isolated from other women as well as from
their male colleagues. In some respects, the feminist academic novels
of the '80s are also the most discouraging and dispiriting about the
prospects for women sharing the joys of the academic life.

The most important feminist academic novel of the decade is
Death in a Tenured Position (1981). As in most of Carolyn Heilbrun's
other "Amanda Cross" novels, her sleuth is Kate Fansler, a professor
of Victorian literature at "one of New York's largest and most prestigious universities" and a sort of "Our Gal Sunday" of the Ivy League.
The ever-willowy Kate makes her appearance, "dressed for the patri-
archy," in a fashionable raincoat, elegant flat-heeled shoes, and an
ultra-suede suit with a gold pin on the lapel.[1] If anyone made a

movie of this novel, I have the horrible suspicion that Kate would be played by Julia Roberts.

It is probably already obvious from what I have said about the earlier novels in the series that I usually find Kate Fansler an obnoxious and intolerable heroine—pompous, stilted, and humorless. I detest the way she throws pretentious quotations into every conversation and uses faux-Britishisms like "shan't." I despise her self-importance and snobbery. I am annoyed by her Jamesian adverb placements— "Why is Jocasta [a dog] so beautifully snoring on my couch?" (12). I hate her hatreds of children and grandchildren, of the word *gay*, of instant coffee, printed cards, and television. But this novel nevertheless struck a personal chord with me; in it Heilbrun begins to talk about the problems plaguing women who had made it in academia and to caution those who had not. Perhaps it stands out because it seems like Heilbrun's most personal novel and, in retrospect, her darkest. Its themes of loneliness, alienation, and self-punishment can be seen as precursors of her own suicide in the fall of 2003.

This time, Kate is at Harvard at the request of Professor Janet Mandelbaum, the first tenured woman in the Harvard English department. Janet has been hired because the English department has received a million-dollar bequest of an endowed position to a woman. One senior member, writing to a friend at Columbia, wonders whether "we could get Iris Murdoch? We could take her respected husband John Bayley, too, a *fine* critic; he could teach the course (husbands must have some rights left) and she could quietly write her novels" (3).

But Janet, a specialist in seventeenth-century poetry, is hired. "At her former university, Janet had turned her back on the whole idea of women; she had operated within her department, had been accepted, at least to her satisfaction, as one of the boys. Telling herself that any woman with qualifications could make it, she had been as strict as any man in judging the women who applied for jobs or tenure. She had come to Harvard full of hope for the same scene, but better; that hope had been harshly denied" (49). Then someone slips something into her drink at a department cocktail party, and she winds up unconscious in the bathtub in the ladies' room with a member of the local lesbian commune. What a scandal! But a member of the group comes to New York to ask Kate for help.

Although she claims to loathe Harvard Square (another strike against her in my book, as one who spent her adolescence in Harvard Square), Kate comes up, ostensibly to annoy her conservative brothers, and stays first at the Harvard Faculty Club, in a room so "uncomfortable and inconvenient" that it must be the result of a "sinister mind at work" (27), then at a place she calls the Institute—Radcliffe's Bunting Institute for research on women. And soon thereafter, Janet Mandelbaum's dead body is discovered in the men's room of Warren House, the English department's home, poisoned by cyanide. Kate naturally attempts to solve the crime.

Heilbrun's author's note to the novel imitated the disclaimers so familiar in British satires. "None of the persons actually appearing in this novel, connected or unconnected with Harvard, bears any resemblance to anyone anywhere. To emphasize the truth of this assertion particularly in regard to Harvard's English department, the author states that she has met a very few tenured members of that department, and is acquainted with only one, who does not appear in this story. The author had entered Warren House only once, uninvited, to case the joint for the purpose of writing this book." In her memoir, she returned to the theme of denial: "When I portrayed some fictional members of the Harvard English department, no one believed they were not portraits of actual Harvard faculty. In fact, as I plainly stated in the front of the book, I knew no one in that department except one man who had moved there from Columbia, and he was not in my novel. Nonetheless, the conviction that these characters were based on life persisted. I came to understand this only with the realization, which was some years in coming, that all pompous, self-satisfied male professors have similar characteristics; if you have described one, you have described them all."[2]

Of course, the characters are fictionalized; but Heilbrun's assertions draw attention to a willful ignorance. Kate Fansler is constantly aggrieved that she is being ignored, neglected, and patronized by the Harvard English faculty: "Great fame in the critical world I do not claim. Still, I have, or thought I had, what my male colleagues call a national reputation" (80). Yet she brags that she doesn't know the names of any of its members. Has she been on the moon? (Actually, she's not being truthful, because she discusses them with a New York colleague before she goes to Cambridge.) Generally, tenured professors in a department at one Ivy League university have some familiarity with their colleagues at the others; and even in the 1970s when it was in a trough between its earlier and its present glory, the Harvard English faculty was well-known. Everyone in the profession who had any kind of savvy at all knew that Helen Vendler and Barbara Lewalski were the tenured women in English at Harvard, the first since the Milton scholar Isabel MacCaffrey, who was the very first and who had been my professor and role model when she taught at Bryn Mawr. Vendler had been president of the MLA in 1980, preceding Heilbrun herself by only four years. Harvard's famous professor of playwriting, "the nicest, most unpompous, kindest most unHarvard person" must be William Alfred. Heilbrun's villain, the feline homosexual Professor Allen Adam Clarkville, who cites Samuel Johnson in his first appearance, sounds a lot like the great Johnson scholar Walter Jackson Bate, one of Harvard's most distinguished curmudgeons, and an open antagonist of deconstruction and feminism. For an English professor, pretending not to know who these people are is like a politician insisting he doesn't know who he is running against.

As she unravels the sad story of Janet Mandelbaum, Kate also seems to be hinting that, for women, life in a tenured position is not as great as it is cracked up to be. Although they are not friends, Janet Mandelbaum resembles Kate Fansler. They have had romances with the same Jewish man, Moon Mandelbaum (he married Janet, he tells Kate, because she was "even more Gentile than you, if you know what I mean"), and they are both beautiful, isolated, and smug. Neither has much interest in feminism. Even before she gets up to Harvard, we see Fansler at her prestigious New York university, the only woman member of a dull committee. "Kate would sometimes picture her tombstone with 'The Token Woman' engraved in the marble" (4). When Janet gets into trouble, she sends for Kate, simply because women her age "who are professors in prestigious universities and know all about what that is like are not exactly legion" (18).

In fact, Kate's position, so much desired and sought, has become dull; she has tenure, to be sure, but she suffers from "survivor guilt" (6). And she explains that she has come to Harvard because she is at a moment of professional crisis and dissatisfaction: "I came, if you want to know, because I'm bored. Whether because we've lost our audience for literature, or because one can't teach *Middlemarch*, not even *Middlemarch*, forever, or because I think the political movements, the social movements, are important now the way the humanities were important when I was beginning to teach. . . . I think what is happening here now, with Janet, matters; I don't think what happens in the English Department in my university matters bloody much, not at present" (58–59). At Harvard, too, she attends an excruciatingly boring faculty seminar on Browning. Heilbrun herself had expressed similar views in 1979, in an essay called "Bringing the Spirit Back to English Studies," in which she described the state of English studies "in a state it would be meiotic to call parlous." When she and "a colleague" (it was Nancy K. Miller) started to teach the novel from a feminist perspective, "a vitality entered the classroom that I had not experienced, I realized, for many years, nor had the students."[3]

Janet Mandelbaum's life is not a happy one either. She is desperately lonely. Before she was hired, the English department professors had her to dinner and were "welcoming and . . . civilized" (40). But when she arrived, the atmosphere changed. Although the men are courteous to her, they are not friendly. Everyone expects her to be a spokeswoman for feminism and women's studies, and Janet, like Kate, is uncomfortable with the feminist community, although it offers support: "hard to stay away, impossible to join" (66). As Kate says about Harvard, "women, at least around here, live in a never-never land, not certain where they belong, where their allegiances lie, not even what their hopes are. It's no different in New York, except that New York itself consists in not belonging, at least for a great many people in it" (63).

Kate discovers that Janet has been publicly humiliated in a department meeting when she is brutally confronted by a colleague impatient with her refusal to teach women's studies: "Since we've got saddled with you, it does seem the least you could do would be to take care of this problem for us" (139). Like Eleanor Marx, whose biography she has been reading, and like Emma Bovary, whose story Eleanor Marx had translated, Mandelbaum, "in despair at having no place to live her life, and no life to live," kills herself (154). It's certainly a strong ending, a memorable ending, a disturbing ending, although not especially realistic. A real-life Janet Mandelbaum would have looked for another job, and found one. But Heilbrun wants to emphasize the futility of human wishes, the impossibility of a woman's ever becoming androgynous, "a full-fledged member of the brotherhood of professors" (82).

Another brilliant woman scholar who thinks of herself as part of that brotherhood and is shocked out of her innocence, is Marya Knauer, in Joyce Carol Oates's novel *Marya: A Life* (1986).[4] Marya, an assistant professor of literature "in a prestigious but rather small old New Hampshire college that had never, in its two-hundred-thirty-year history, awarded any woman tenure or promoted her to a higher rank" (234), is a grim workaholic, committed to the academic life in the romantic and naive belief that it is genderless: "Knowledge itself was genderless . . . the scholarly life was genderless" (186). She is "the good girl, the A-plus student, fired by competition and virtually inexhaustible" (223).

Marya believes that an obsession with tenure is a masculine one; she herself is immune to it. "She worked very hard and thrived on it, was invigorated by it, uncomplaining, zealous, filled with ideas about how to organize her classes, how to draw out her quieter students, how to . . . make her way in this extraordinary phase of her life. Because she was new on the staff she hadn't the immediate pressures of promotion and tenure to deal with; she even thought it rather petty, rather *vulgar* of certain of her colleagues to spend so much time in careerist speculation" (242). Meanwhile she publishes away—articles and reviews in addition to a well-received scholarly book.

On the day of the departmental tenure review, Marya goes for a bicycle ride with her lover, Gregory, another assistant professor with a book on Yeats from Oxford University Press and a work in progress on Pound's *Cantos*. They have agreed to ignore the impending decision. Somehow though, Gregory increases the speed, turns the picnic into a race; and Marya, although she thinks of herself as noncompetitive, struggles to keep up with him rather than to admit weakness or drop out. Finally she crashes her bike. In the café where she is resting, Gregory breaks their pact and telephones the department to discover she got tenure and he didn't. Marya is so brilliant that she can ignore the tensions of academic rivalry, but her immunity from the harsh realities of the profession make her as unrealistic a model as Janet Mandelbaum.

Alison Lurie's *Foreign Affairs* (1984) focuses on another woman in a tenured position, but where Heilbrun is self-dramatizing and Oates is ironic, Lurie is mercilessly satirical to the pretensions of her heroine. Vinnie Miner is on sabbatical from Corinth, her upstate New York Ivy League university, to carry out research in England on children's folklore. The sabbatical is always a time for reflection and renewal, and like many English professors, Vinnie is in love "with England as well as with her literature."[5] Also in London is her young colleague Fred Turner (the son of Emily and Holman Turner from *Love and Friendship*), an assistant professor at Corinth studying John Gay. He is a handsome young man with his mother's good looks, and so he too has had trouble with the department: "He was suspected, quite unfairly, of being vain, self-centered, unintellectual, and unserious" (30).

But Vinnie's sabbatical begins badly: on the plane she reads a nasty article about her project by L. D. Zimmern, a professor and critic at Columbia. Vinnie already feels like the Cinderella of her department, where she is unmarried, aging, plain, and working in an unfashionable field. "Within the departmental family she sits in the chimney-corner, while her idle, ugly siblings dine at the chairman's table—though, to judge by enrollment figures, many of them must spout toads and lizards" (6–7). She imagines them all gleefully reading Zimmern's essay. But of course she must never show any pain: "In academic life it is considered weak and undignified to complain of your reviews. Indeed . . . the only afflictions it is really safe to mention are those shared by all your colleagues: the weather, inflation, delinquent students, and so forth" (9). Vinnie has some qualities in common with Kate Fansler, especially her intellectual and social snobbery; but Lurie's novel is far more satisfying because she takes an ironic perspective on her heroine. In particular, Vinnie is accompanied everywhere by an invisible dog: "Her familiar demon or demon familiar, known to her privately as Fido and representing self-pity" (3). Fido lets out a woof whenever Vinnie broods on her lack of fame or the slights she receives from her colleagues.

L. D. Zimmern does not make an appearance in the novel, although it turns out that his daughter is Fred Turner's wife. But Zimmern is one of the first feisty academic Jewish figures to star in the '80s *Professorroman*. And it is no accident that he teaches at

Columbia (where Kate Fansler seems not to notice him). In *The Mind-Body Problem* (1983), Rebecca Goldstein compares the ethnicity of Columbia and Princeton:

> My views on The Life of the Mind had been modeled on the people I had known at Columbia: urban intellectuals, unkempt, graceless, morose creatures who walked around with eyes downcast, muttering to themselves. Those were the sorts of bodies—neglected, misshapen, decaying—that serious minds belonged in. But here were these first-rate thinkers who worried about their backyards and backhands, who discussed Buber and black holes over barbeques. The genteel goyishness of the place overwhelmed me. There were Jews at Princeton, of course, but nobody *seemed* Jewish. At Columbia even the non-Jews had seemed Jewish.[6]

Other mystery novels with feminist academic detectives followed Heilbrun's lead. In England, Joan Smith's Loretta Lawson made her debut, in 1987, in *A Masculine Ending*.[7] A leftwing feminist journalist and veteran author of many mystery novels, Smith saw the thematic possibilities of conflicts within feminism as a plot. In the novel, Lawson, who lectures in English literature at London University, goes to Paris to give a paper at an international symposium on recent developments in feminist thought, sponsored by *Fem Sap*, a journal of feminist literary criticism. Presumably the journal's title is an allusion to *Homo sapiens* and not sappy women. But Lawson expects some "intemperate and robust arguments." She belongs to the journal's editorial collective, but "schisms arose endlessly among the various alliances formed by European and American feminists, and on this occasion she anticipated a heated exchange on how to deal with the problem of masculine grammatical forms." The French feminists and the Anglo-American feminists usually come to blows over language and gender; but this time, although the symposium is sisterly, Lawson finds that a murder has been committed in the flat she is using. (Thrifty and impecunious British academics borrow or rent flats when they travel, rather than staying in expensive hotels, as Americans going to the MLA do.) The mystery is resolved when the novel ends in another *Fem Sap* meeting in Paris. The "row over masculine endings" has escalated to open battle, with the radicals determined that all nouns and verb endings in French and Italian should be treated as feminine and threatening to split off and start a new journal called *Mother Tongue*. But of course the "masculine ending" of the title refers ironically both to the solution of the crime— no grammar-crazed feminist is the murderer—and the unstressed denouement—a feminine ending.

Don DeLillo's *White Noise* has all the trappings of the academic novel, but it is also a postmodernist tour de force.[8] DeLillo's novel is set at the College-on-the-Hill, which mirrors John Winthrop's vision of puritan America, a moral beacon to the world. The department heads at the college wear robes like friars or priests: "not grand sweeping full-length affairs but sleeveless tunics puckered at the shoulders." The students may bask in "a romance of human consciousness, as they witness the chairman walking across campus, crook'd arm emerging from his medieval robe, the digital watch blinking in late summer dusk. The robe is black, of course, and goes with almost anything" (9).

His narrator, Jack Gladney, is the chairman of the Department of Hitler Studies. "I invented Hitler studies in North America in March of 1968. It was a cold bright day with intermittent winds out of the east. When I suggested to the chancellor that we might build a whole department around Hitler's life and work, he was quick to see the possibilities. It was an immediate and electrifying success" (4). Gladney's office is in Centenary Hall, along with the popular culture department, officially called American environments, and DeLillo's description of the department prefigures characters and ideas that would become staples of the academic novel. The chairman, Alphonse (Fast Food) Stompanato is a "broad-chested, glowering man" who collects prewar soda pop bottles. His faculty, "New York émigrés, smart, thuggish, movie-mad, trivia-crazed," are "male, wear rumpled clothes, need haircuts, cough into their armpits. Together they look like teamster officials assembled to identify the body of a mutilated colleague" (9).

One of these émigrés is Murray Jay Siskind, the itinerant lecturer in "American icons" who speaks for the author's mordant point of view. Murray regards himself as a paradigmatic Jewish academic, the wandering Jew of film noir. He is the Jewish academic as moral and theoretical spokesman prefigured by Morris Zapp and Roth's professors of desire and sorrow. Murray is a "stoop-shouldered man with little round glasses" (10) who dresses exclusively in corduroy and lives in a gothic rooming house, which is the site of archetypally unhappy lives. As the Jew in this assemblage, he pontificates on meaning and its absence; and yet he is not in the least perturbed by Hitler studies. Gladney, as Siskind admiringly tells him, has put his mark on the field: "Nobody on the faculty of any college or university in this part of the country can so much as utter the word Hitler without a nod in your direction, literally or metaphorically. This is the center, the unquestioned source. He is now your Hitler, Gladney's Hitler" (11–12). Siskind aspires to do the same with Elvis studies.

DeLillo's deadpan account of Hitler and Elvis studies sounds like a hilarious parody of academic fashion in the '80s; that lethal phrase, "in this part of the country," is a wonderful put-down of Gladney's pretensions to national reputation. Moreover, Gladney has invented an extra initial and renamed himself J. A. K. Gladney in an effort to give his work more gravitas, just as many academics in the '80s and '90s suddenly began to sign themselves with three names. He gains weight and sports glasses with "thick heavy black frames and dark lenses" to invest Hitler studies with "dignity, significance and prestige" (17). In one of the novel's many duels of popular-culture combat, Gladney visits Siskind's Elvis seminar to riff on Hitler in a bravura performance: "It was not a small matter. We all have an aura to maintain, and in sharing mine with a friend I was risking the very things that made me untouchable" (74).

DeLillo has denied that he meant to satirize higher education: "This isn't a campus novel, and it's not a satire on college life. And as far as I'm concerned, they did get decent educations. I don't think this was a issue at all . . . this is just a comment on the kind of superspecialization that has entered our culture in the last 15 years or so. Why not an academic specialty devoted to a single individual, if the individual is as important as Hitler."[9] Of course he does satirize the campus, but in the interests of something larger, so that *White Noise* is in the category of great American fiction about the soul. It is about the fear of death and the ways people stave it off with knowledge, titles, robes, and ceremonies. These meanings emerge in the processions, the versions of convocation and commencement, birth and death, with which DeLillo frames the book, in an ironic style that returns these moments on the academic calendar to their religious and monastic roots. First, an ironic celebration of the fall season:

> The station wagons arrived at noon, a long shining line that coursed through the west campus. In single file they eased around the orange I-beam sculpture and moved toward the dormitories. The roofs of the station wagons were loaded down with carefully secured suitcases full of light and heavy clothing; with boxes of blankets, boots and shoes, stationery and books, sheets, pillows, quilts ... the objects inside; the stereo sets, radios, personal computers; small refrigerators and table ranges; the cartons of phonograph records and cassettes; the hairdryers and styling irons; the tennis rackets, soccer balls, hockey and lacrosse sticks, bows and arrows; the controlled substances, the birth control pills and devices, the junk food still in shopping bags . . . Waffelos and Kabooms, fruit chews and toffee popcorn; the Dum-Dum pops, the Mystic mints. (3)

The last procession is funereal. At the end of the novel, having survived a mysterious toxic disaster and a marital crisis, the Gladneys are shopping at the supermarket. In a brilliantly condensed parable, one of the most haunting and masterful passages in American fiction, DeLillo presents the consumer check-out line as a metaphor for the American way of spirituality and death:

> And this is where we wait together, regardless of age, our carts stocked with brightly-colored goods. A slowly moving line, satisfying, giving us time to glance at the tabloids in the racks. Everything we need that is not food or love is here in the tabloid racks. The tales of the supernatural and the extraterrestrial. The miracle vitamins, the cures for cancer, the remedies for obesity. The cults of the famous and the dead. (326)

The academic cults of the famous and the dead were also brought to the attention of a wide-reading public in 1984, with the publication of David Lodge's comic novel, *Small World*. Behind the jokes of the novel are the academic transformations of the star system in literary studies. As David R. Shumway described it, "The emergence of academic stars . . . marks a fundamental shift in the profession of literary studies. . . . Professors are suddenly suffused with a glamour usually reserved for public celebrities." Shumway dates the beginning of the shift to an article in the *New York Times Magazine* in 1986, on "The Tyranny of the Yale Critics," but he acknowledges that "the most important catalyst for the emergence of academic stars is the conference and lecture circuit."[10] And of course, Lodge had anticipated the mass media's recognition of academic celebrity culture through his own experience as a traveling theorist. *Small World*, he told me, was "set in 1979, when I first got the idea for it at the James Joyce symposium in Zurich, with all these scholars converging from all over the world and meeting in the James Joyce Pub and making arrangements to go jogging. . . . I think the pilgrimage analogy was that, well, nominally you were there for sort of spiritual reasons, you were cultivating your mind and meeting your colleagues to discuss scholarly matters. But it was also fun—this kind of party was going on."[11]

Moreover, Stanley Fish and other jet-setters were discussing the conference scene long before it became a *New Yorker* cartoon. "Flying down to Charlottesville," Fish said, "is just an ordinary piece of business in the life of many academics. By 'Charlottesville' I don't mean that all conferences are in Charlottesville, but I mean that people regularly go to conferences. It's really a phenomenon, and it has changed the structure of the way in which we do business."[12]

The annual meeting of the MLA was the biggest and most publicized of these conferences, and by the early 1980s, it was being described, not just in English and American, but even in French academic novels, as sexy and arousing, as well as a form of business. In *Un amour de soi* (1982), a roman à clef by Serge Doubrovsky, the convention is

officially . . . a job market, a slave auction. Rumors, X *has got a job in Texas*, whispers, *I think that at Harvard*. The six thousand professors who swoop down for three days, stingers ready, swirling like bees, have come to make their honey. In the hive, a high. On thirty floors, in a hundred cells, each to his own honeycomb. Specialized by language, by literature, by century, by genre, by author, by work, by chapter, by paragraph. Everyone has his twenty-minute scholarly say, swarms of culture, the testing ground. The stars perorate, the well-off strut. The losers come just to show up. . . . All together, they collect the nectar of knowledge. They connect, too, a little, a lot, pell-mell, male, female, crushed in, stifling corridors, packed halls, from morning to evening, from session to session, sitting, standing, by dint of rubbing against each other, they mingle. Overheated spaces, that overexcites you. Hard to get through the hallway, you get a hard-on.[13]

David Lodge reflects on this covert mixture of excitements in the itineraries of professional advancement in his novel *Small World* (1984), which he has described as "a novel about desire, and not just sexual desire but also the desire to succeed; I conceived it as an academic comedy of manners which would have a romance plot underneath it, and in some ways the two elements are incompatible. Satire is the antithesis of romance, because romance is ultimately about the achievement of desire; satire is saying that you won't get what you desire, you don't deserve it."[14]

The novel begins in April, the season of pilgrimages, or conferences, at a tiny conference at Rummidge. "The modern conference," Lodge writes, "resembles the pilgrimages of medieval Christendom in that it allows the participants to indulge themselves in all the pleasures and diversions of travel while appearing to be austerely bent on self-improvement."[15] Indeed, I used to be amazed at the stoicism and obtuseness of many of my colleagues, who persisted in treating the conference as a chore to be manfully completed, rather than a networking opportunity. But the Rummidge, or British conference, does not satisfy these ends, for it offers no pleasures and few diversions. In this initial poor excuse for a conference, Lodge's fictional superstar Morris Zapp appears to instruct young Persse McGarrigle, the novice English professor who is the hero of the pilgrimage/romance plot, in the basic rules of conference-going:

1. "Never go to lectures. Unless you're giving one yourself, of course. Or *I'm* giving one" (18).
2. The conference circuit has replaced both the university and the department as the unit of professionalization. "Scholars don't have to work in the same institution to interact, nowadays: they call each other up, or they meet at international conferences. . . . A young man in a hurry can see the world by conference-hopping" (43–44).

3. "Food and accommodation are the most important things about any conference. If the people are happy with *those*, they'll generate intellectual excitement" (65).
4. "It is impossible to be excessive in flattery of one's peers" (152).
5. "Nobody pays to get laid at a conference" (237).

Other rules of the conference will emerge over the course of the book, as Persse flies from London to Amsterdam to Lausanne to Los Angeles to Tokyo to New York in quest of a beautiful graduate student named Angelica. Meanwhile Morris Zapp, also aloft and in many cities and with many adventures, defends the joys of academic life, but on a different scale: "The day of the single static campus is over. And the single, static campus novel with it" (63). Zapp is a candidate for the UNESCO Chair of Literary Criticism, which carries a big salary and no teaching responsibilities, the Holy Grail of Academe, and Lodge uses the plot device of the competitive quest to satirize several of the leading schools and practitioners of High Theory.

But the '80s are also the age of feminism, and although only one female theorist, a Julia Kristeva figure with the Arthurian-sounding name of Fulvia Morgana, is a candidate for the chair, Lodge gives the final statement in the novel to Angelica, who offers a critique of the structure of traditional narrative, ending with a "single, explosive discharge of accumulated tension," an "essentially *male* climax" (322), even if it is an event involving a heroine, like the suicides of Emma Bovary, Barbara Kirk, or Janet Mandelbaum. Instead, Angelica proposes a different kind of narrative, a romance, with detached episodes that could recur ad infinitum and in which "the pleasure of this text comes and comes and comes again. . . . Romance is a multiple orgasm" (322–23).

This romance model, indeed, would come to dominate the writing of academic fiction with a specifically feminist agenda. Carol Shields wrote repeatedly of the fragility and historical contingency of women's lives, even when those lives seem outwardly placid and safe. One of her favorite techniques was to juxtapose a contemporary woman writer or professor with a mythic female figure from the past. In her extraordinary novel *Swann* (1987), Shields wrote about Sarah Maloney, a feminist professor of English who teaches courses on

American women poets and "Women in Midwestern Fiction." Maloney has made a crossover success with her Ph.D. thesis, *The Female Prism*, which became a best-seller; and she has discovered the poetry of an obscure Canadian woman named Mary Swann, becoming her feminist academic champion. Now Swann is becoming an industry and a cult figure, and academics, librarians, and collectors are fighting over her possession.

In the structure of the novel, Shields tells both the story of Mary Swann, an abused rural housewife murdered by her husband, and the story of her art, as it is seen through the eyes of the academics who want to own her, the local woman who befriended her, and the small-town editor/publisher who, we learn, more or less reconstructed her poems from fragments after her death. At a symposium—a conference observing all of Zapp's Laws—which ends the novel, narrated as a film script, the academics gathered to analyze Swann end up themselves reconstituting her work from memory after all known copies have vanished. Combining a grisly realism with a surreal, postmodern account of how poetry is created, interpreted, given value, and launched as art, *Swann* is a spectacular achievement. Shields invents Mary Swann's poetry as well:

Blood pronounces my name
Blisters the day with shame
Spends what little I own,
Robbing the hour, rubbing the bone.[16]

While she empathizes with several male and female characters, Shields puts Sarah Maloney at the novel's center, and Sarah is a successful academic woman who is also trying to work out the details of her life, including relationships with men. The only aspect of the book that is disappointing is Sarah's impatience with the academy, with "the pretensions. The false systems. The arcane lingo. The macho domination. The garrison mentality. The inbred arrogance" (21). She is a player, a winner; but she doesn't want to play and she doesn't want to win.

Ironically, the most detailed, convincing, and upbeat portrait of the feminist academic in the '80s comes from a novel by a man: David Lodge's *Nice Work* (1988).[17] The story of *Nice Work* begins on

January 13, 1986, as Vic Wilcox and Robyn Penrose are waking up for their respective work. Robyn is a temporary lecturer in English at the University of Rummidge. She unites theory and feminism. Vic is the managing director of J. Pringle and Sons Casting & General Engineering Company in West Wallsbury, which supplies parts to the motor industry. Robyn and Vic are asked to participate in a "Shadow Scheme," connecting the university with industry. She learns the business point of view on strikes, women's labor, automation, unemployment, and venture capital. He learns about literary theory and feminism, and these subjects are more relevant to his life than we might suppose. In short, the novel is a kind of *Changing Places* between the factory and the university, the business world and the learning society.

On one very explicit level, the book is based on the English industrial novel, especially Elizabeth Gaskell's *North and South* (1854–55). Gaskell's novel contrasted the north and south of England as being almost two nations, one rich and the other working-class; Lodge contrasts the elitism of the university with the democratic roar of the factory. But an equally important theme of Gaskell's book is the loss of faith: an Anglican clergyman, Reverend Hale, tells his daughter Margaret that he must resign his comfortable parish in the south of England: "I must no longer be a minister in the Church of England." Hale feels unable to "make a fresh declaration of conformity to the Liturgy at my institution," so he cannot accept a promotion and he feels that it is cowardly and false to stay where he is.[18]

Similarly, *Nice Work* is about the loss of academic faith and whether the professor who has stopped believing in the sacred codes and liturgies of literary theory (or whatever) should also move on. Teaching in a university is nice work, to be sure, especially compared to working in a factory; but it entails certain commitments of faith and allegiance, and under the conditions of academic hard times that Lodge describes, not everyone can conscientiously remain.

Robyn is a true believer. The daughter of a prosperous professor with a personal chair on the south coast of England, she has been an undergraduate at Sussex, where, "as bright young people often did in the 1970s," she read Marx and Freud and lost her virginity (23); we might think of her as a student of Howard Kirk or someone like him. When she gets a First in Literature, she decides to go to Cambridge:

Intellectually, it was an exciting time to be a research student in the English Faculty. New ideas imported from Paris by the more adventurous young teachers glittered like dustmotes in the Fenland air; structuralism and poststructuralism, semiotics and deconstruction, new mutations and graftings of psychoanalysis and Marxism, linguistics and literary criticism. The more conservative dons viewed these ideas and their proponents with alarm, seeing in them a threat to the traditional values and methods of literary scholarship. Battle was joined, in seminars, lectures, committee meetings and the review pages of scholarly journals. It was revolution. It was civil war. (26)

Robyn joins in the struggle; her eyes becomes bloodshot reading Lacan and Kristeva; she continually revises her thesis on the industrial novel to keep up with all theoretical shifts.

Then in 1981, all hell broke loose in the Cambridge English Faculty. An extremely public row about the denial of tenure to a young lecturer associated with the progressive party opened old wounds and inflicted new ones on the always thin-skinned community. . . . For a few weeks, the controversy featured in the national and even international press, up-market newspapers carrying spicy stories about the leading protagonists and confused attempts to explain the difference between structuralism and post-structuralism to the man on the Clapham omnibus. To Robyn it seemed that critical theory had at last moved to its rightful place, centre-stage, in the theatre of history. (27)

But the moment passes; Margaret Thatcher starts cutting higher education; and "the previously unthinkable prospect of a non-academic career now began to be thought—with fear, dismay, and bewilderment on Robyn's part. Of course she was aware, cognitively, that there was a life outside universities, but she knew nothing about it. . . . When she tried to imagine herself working in an office or a bank, her mind soon went blank, like a cinema screen when the projector breaks down or the film snaps" (29).

A product of the '80s theory generation, Robyn, unlike Jane Clifford in *The Odd Woman*, no longer believes in the unified "self"; she thinks there is no such thing, "only a subject position in an infinite web of discourses" (21–22); and rather than being in love, she admits having once "allowed myself to be constructed by the discourse of romantic love for a while" (210). But of course Robyn behaves as if she had a unified self, and Lodge gives an exact portrait of her styles and habits, from her chic Habitat retro alarm clock, *muesli*, and Laura Ashley nightgown to her subscriptions to *Tel Quel* and *Critical Inquiry*. She is in every way a model postmodern feminist academic.

But when she starts to shadow Vic at the factory, she actually begins to change. "She now had this other life on one day of the week, and almost another identity. . . . It was as if the Robyn Penrose who spent one day a week at the factory was the shadow of the self who on the other six days a week was busy with women's studies and post-structuralist literary theory—less substantial, more elusive, but just as real. She led a double life these days, and felt herself to be a more interesting and complex person because of it" (151). But rather than losing her faith and leaving the university, as some of her friends do, Robyn sees that higher education should not have to defend or justify itself in utilitarian terms, but should be more democratic and open to everyone.

Morris Zapp appears as the Jewish deus ex machina, touching down at Rummidge to be the guest of the Swallows. He and Robyn have a conversation in which "the names of prominent feminist critics and theorists crackled between them like machine-gun fire: Elaine Showalter [my fifteen minutes of fame], Sandra Gilbert, Susan Gubar, Shoshana Felman, Luce Irigaray, Catherine Clément, Susan Suleiman, Mieke Bal—Morris Zapp had read them all" (234). Zapp gets Euphoria State University Press to bid on Robyn's book, advises Robyn to ask for an advance twice as big as they propose (I have heard from friends that Fish often proffers financial advice to other professors, gratis, for the sheer love of bargaining), and invites her to apply for a job at Euphoria.

Nevertheless the postmodern Robyn shares the traditionalist C. P. Snow's view of the university as a utopia, or as the idea of a utopia. Looking out over the campus lawn in the summer, she thinks that "the university was the ideal type of a human community, where work and play, culture and nature, were in perfect harmony, where there was space and light, and fine buildings set in pleasant grounds, and people were free to pursue excellence and self-fulfillment, each according to her own rhythm and inclination" (249). If the factory could come to the university, she imagines, if "the values of the university and the imperatives of commerce" could be reconciled, the whole of society would be improved (250). Like a heroine in the industrial novel, Robyn gets an unexpected legacy, and she decides to stay at Rummidge to follow her faith and to lend Vic the money to start an enlightened business of his own.

I'm not at all sure I believe in this happy ending, but I derive multiple pleasures from reading about it.

chapter 5

∽

The Nineties

TENURED TOWERS

B Y THE 1990S, and through the end of the century, the lottery of hiring, political correctness, the culture wars, and the tragedies of tenure had become familiar topics in academic fiction, wearing away the last vestiges of idealism. "I couldn't believe it," says a character in *The Ticking Tenure Clock* (1998). "Walter Kravitz had been denied tenure, and denied at the lowest level of review. He had not even had the opportunity to be swatted down by the dreaded dean's committee, which could and often did overturn a department's favorable recommendation."[1] In another novel, *Gaveston* (2002), the academic heroine muses wryly on her research: "The same fundamental formula: 'Desperate for Tenure: A Meaningless Rehashing of a Subject on which Everything Has Already Been Said but Necessary to Secure My Degree/Teaching Post/ Continuing Academic Status/Chances of Reviewing for the TLS.'"[2]

By the turn of the century, English departments had become the locus for the greatest disappointment and frustration. According to Shannon Olson, in *Welcome to My Planet* (2000),

> The English Department is sandwiched into two hallways, surrounded by science and engineering students, recognizable by their calculators and sense of purpose. No one knows what to do with English anymore, where it fits, "a capacious field," the chair of our department calls it at our spring quarter assembly, then he makes a joke about Milton that everyone responds to with clench-jawed laughs. I look around for donuts, which are unlikely. The English Department,

from what I can tell, is given all the bad office equipment and old furniture, while the business students, the medical students, the engineering students, move one school of study at a time into new buildings with green-tinted glass. The students in our capacious field are recognizable for . . . their looks of ennui and hopelessness. If they are lucky, they will get jobs in other neglected English departments in Alaska, Tennessee or South Dakota.[3]

The various roles English departments offer their faculty had also come to the center of both the novel and the profession. Hazard Adams had labeled some of these roles in his book of advice on academic tribes. After tenure, "the faculty member learns that he must not find but make his role. He then sets to work carving and painting a suitable array of masks. There are, of course, many roles (shaman, monk, organizer, guru, orator, entrepreneur, to name a few)."[4] Another department chairman had compared them to the roles in a family: "Who will be the bad father, favorite son, dutiful daughter, garrulous uncle, mischievous cousin? Who will be the brother cheated out of his birthright, nurturing mother, doddering granddad? Who the querulous child, the indulged crazy, the keeper of the flame?"[5] In the 1990s, as academic novels proliferated, most satirized this new cast of characters and their struggles for tenure, status, and political correctness; the tone of these books is much more vituperative, vengeful, and cruel than in earlier decades. In contrast to David Lodge's cheery portrait in *Small World* of the festive New York MLA as the Big Daddy of conferences, D. J. H. Jones's *Murder at the MLA* (1993) is set in Chicago, the "the mean streets of MLA."[6] I don't know the identity of the pseudonymous D. J. H. Jones. On the book's cover he is described as "a reconstructed New Critic, [who has had] brief incarnations as a deconstructionist, Marxist-feminist, postmodernist, and poststructuralist, but now firmly denies any critical allegiance." Certainly Jones has it in for Princeton, with its "arch, affected Princetonian air that can seem so often like an adhesive membrane over the lives of its graduates" (41). Princeton, he writes, is "a Lake Forest kind of place. . . . Not a pinch of dust, even on the fence around the train station. No pigeons, either, but you never see the exterminator. Squeaky clean" (43). At the MLA, he alleges, Princeton tests interviewees with their management of coffee. "Princeton uses another trick, of never asking the candidate any important questions. As a way of off-balancing the candidate to see how well he or she can socialize, just a little chat will happen, confusing and aloof" (80).

In Princeton's defense, I can guarantee that these rumors are false. The fence around the "Dinky" station is filthy, so are the numerous legally protected pigeons, and our MLA practice was as haphazard as everyone else's. One year when I was interviewing, our coffee pot lid became stuck, and one search committee member, a medievalist, rashly offered a job to the next candidate to successfully open it, like pulling forth Excalibur. We had to backtrack quickly on that one.

The first murder victim at the MLA is Susan Engleton, chair of the Wellesley English department, "dead as her prose" (1). Indeed, women department chairs were marked out as murder victims in many '90s books, although tenured women who are found dead were viewed less as tragic martyrs than as job vacancies. Other vaguely familiar composites appear, including Professor Joan Mellish at the Marxist Cash Bar, "the Ultimate Trendy," who specializes in anal eroticism and lives with a gay man (127). Jobs and tenure are more arousing issues than sex, however. A Princeton Ph.D. named Nancy Cook explains the system to the detective investigating the crime: "What you hope is that you won't turn into a little academic Kelly girl. You hope the school's name will look good on your resumé later. You hope you can get a book written fast enough that you can get another job. You try to counter-manipulate the fact of your being manipulated" (41).

Affirmative action and political correctness came in for their share of mockery. Ishmael Reed's *Japanese by Spring* (1993) is one of the very few academic novels written by an African American.[7] Benjamin "Chappie" Puttbutt, a Ph.D. with a dissertation on the 1920s expatriate black poet Nathan Brown, becomes a black neo-con and publishes an article in *New York Exegesis* "denouncing affirmative action."[8] He gets a tenure track job in the English department at Jack London College where racist students run wild, and he curries favor by turning the other cheek. "Puttbutt," writes Reed, "was a member of the growing anti-affirmative action industry. A black pathology merchant. Throw together a three-hundred-page book with graphs and articles about illegitimacy, welfare dependency, single-family households, drugs and violence; paint the inner cities as the circles of hell in the American paradise . . . and you could write your way to the top of the best-seller list. . . . It was the biggest literary hustle going . . . [and] would get him tenure" (10). The premise of the novel, although extreme, is original, but very soon Reed himself began to take up more and more space preaching and ranting against feminism, among other contemporary evils.

John L'Heureux's *The Handmaid of Desire* (1996) is also extreme, punitive, and harsh.[9] Set in a university that is clearly Stanford, it describes the war between the theoretical young Turks and the traditional old Fools, who are all in their fifties and still love literature. Zachary Kurtz, the most aggressive and pugnacious of the young Turks, and a kind of rabid Morris Zapp, explains:

> The faculty breaks down into two camps, along generational lines, but not totally. . . . And the one joining them, the butch one, that's Maddy Barker. A star theorist. Gynocritic of nunneries in the Fourteenth Century. Appropriate if you ask me, but she's good. Very big career, very touchy. Gay, of course. And then there's Concepcion. She's gay, too, but they don't get along. Concepcion teaches Chicana Lit—please note, Chican*a* not Chican*o*—and Barthes and gender stuff. And Leroy O'Shea, he's the Black, he teaches African American and African Anglophone, but he's okay. He's pretty good and tending toward really good. So the Chicanos and the Blacks are good. And we'll be hiring an Indian next year and maybe an Eskimo. We've got the multicultural bag sewed up. (30)

Kurtz plans to take over the English department, dissolve it, and create a new department of "Theory and Discourse."

> It would include Comp Lit, Mod Thought, and all the little language departments—French, Russian, Spanish, you name it. It would take on all written documents, equally and with absolute indifference to the author's reputation or the western canon or the nature of the writing itself—whether it was Flaubert's *Bovary* or a 1950 tax form or the label on a Campbell's soup can; are you following me?—and subject them all to the probing, thrusting, hard-breathing analysis of the latest developments in metaphilosophical literary theory. Whatever these theories might be. Wherever they might lead. (43)

Of course, in his secret boudoir, Kurtz reads Jane Austen; and his Machiavellian schemes are cruelly if justly punished and emasculated by L'Heureux.

James Hynes's *Publish and Perish: Three Tales of Tenure and Terror* (1997) is less malicious and more inventive. In "Queen of the Jungle," Paul has a non–tenure track position in the English department at the State University of Iowa in Bluff City, but his book runs into bad luck—the reader's report is "a career-destroying masterpiece of condescension and mean-spirited wit."[10] Meanwhile his wife, Elizabeth, is doing well and is up for early tenure at Chicago; if he can submit his best chapter—on Kafka and *jouissance*—maybe she can wangle him a job. But Paul can't even revise; he is full of guilt about his affair with a grad student in communications named Kym, and instead he just fills up the screen with gibberish: "dirty limericks, multilingual puns, the lyrics of TV theme songs" (44). Elizabeth prints it out, and of course it makes a huge impression on Chicago. Elizabeth admits that "frankly, it was a little too Andrew Ross for me, but Walter loved it, called it *very* cutting-edge" (49). If he can rewrite the whole manuscript in this vein, he may have a job. Paul sets frenetically to work, throwing in a manic mix of pop references. But he reckons without his wife's cat, Charlotte, who has been watching his affair with Kym and manages first to erase his entire file and then to betray him.

The high point of academic fiction of the 1990s, a book that raised expectations of the literary quality of the entire genre, was A. S. Byatt's *Possession: A Romance*, which received the Booker Prize for 1990. *Possession* is about the intellectual and romantic passion of two young British scholars of Victorian poetry who become obsessed with the mysteries and textual consequences of a secret love affair between Randolph Henry Ash (a cross between Tennyson and Browning) and Christabel LaMotte (half Christina Rossetti, half Emily Dickinson). The novel has a strong element of anti-American satire as well; the British scholars believe that "British writing should stay in Britain and be studied by the British."[11] In other words, they should literally possess their literary treasures and fight off the interloping, conniving, even grave-robbing Americans who come waving checkbooks from ridiculous places in the Southwest.

As a "romance," *Possession* follows up on the elements of quest, multiple plots, and diffuse narrative pleasure that David Lodge had predicted in *Small World*. In its themes of academic competition over art and theft of manuscripts, it suggests Carol Shield's *Swann*, and like Shields, Byatt uncannily re-created the style of Victorian writing in the poems and letters she invented for her characters. "My mind has been full since childhood of the rhythms of Tennyson and Browning, Rossetti and Keats," she has commented. "I read and reread Emily Dickinson, whose harsher and more skeptical voice I found more exciting than Christina Rossetti's meek resignation. I wanted a *fierce* female voice. And I found I was possessed—it was actually quite frightening—the nineteenth-century poems that were not nineteenth-century poems *wrote themselves*, hardly blotted, fitting into the metaphorical structure of my novel, but not mine, as my prose is mine." Byatt got the idea for the novel "in the British Library, watching that great Coleridge scholar, Kathleen Coburn, circumambulating the catalogue. I thought: she has given all her life to *his* thoughts, and then I thought: she has mediated his thoughts to me. And then I thought: Does he possess her, or does she possess him? There could be a novel called *Possession* about the relations between living and dead minds." As her concept evolved, "possession" also become a metaphor for ownership and obsession, economic and sexual.[12]

The Victorian poets in *Possession* are fascinating, especially for me as a Victorianist; but I am mainly intrigued by its academic background and Byatt's take on the world of literary scholarship. The male protagonist, Roland, works in the British Museum and the London Library as part-time research assistant to Professor James Blackadder, his dissertation supervisor, who is editing the complete works of Ash. Blackadder is a Casaubon figure, a gray and dusty man, and his "Ash Factory" is housed in the infernal bowels of the British Museum, "a hot place of metal cabinets and glass cells containing the clatter of typewriters, gloomily lit by neon tubes. Micro-readers glowed green in its gloom. It smelled occasionally sulphurous, when the photocopiers shortcircuited" (31). A victim of the times, like Lodge's Persse, or Hynes's Paul, Roland "would have advanced rapidly and involuntarily" in the "expansive sixties"; instead, he sees himself as cast into hell, a "failure" (14). Part of the novel's fairy-tale plot is the rescue of Roland, an Orpheus in reverse, when he finds—and steals—some lost letters linking Ash to LaMotte.

In contrast to Roland is the thrusting young academic Fergus Wolff, "a child of the Sixties" who had sat at the feet of Barthes and Foucault. Fergus sends Roland to consult the major LaMotte expert, Dr. Maud Bailey, who directs the Women's Resource Centre at Lincoln University. Lincoln has all the characteristics of imaginary universities in the British academic novel, "white-tiled towers" (44), a glass-walled library, and a paternoster lift—an open elevator with a series of chambers that revolves slowly, an image of the cyclical nature of academic time. Maud herself is a green girl, a beautiful, statuesque, unsmiling amazon who always dresses in green and white, and wears a silk turban around her long blond hair. She is the princess in the glassy tower, and she and Roland fall in love, although, like Lodge's Robyn, they belong to critical generations that do not believe in love. Together they solve the mystery of the secret affair between Ash and LaMotte and defeat the voracious American interlopers who try to buy the manuscripts. Roland gets job offers from universities in Hong Kong, Barcelona, and Amsterdam, and in the spirit of the '90s, they will commute. As in *Nice Work*, this is a happy and affirmative ending: the academic life is worth living, worth making sacrifices for; studying the past and immersing oneself in its literature is a profoundly satisfying way of life and not a substitute for, or an obstacle to, life.

Byatt, however, is ambivalent about the feminist literary scholarship that makes her story of the recovery and reinterpretation of a Victorian woman poet possible. On one hand, she celebrates and defends the older generation of women scholars who might have benefited from the women's movement. As Beatrice Nest, a representative of this generation, tells Maud: "I don't think you can imagine, Miss Bailey, how it was then. We were dependent and excluded persons. In my early days—indeed until the late 1960s—women were *not permitted* to enter the main Senior Common Room. . . . Everything was decided in the pub—everything of import—where we were not invited and did not wish to go. . . . We were grateful for employment" (240–41).

On the other hand, the only parodic character in the book is the

American feminist critic Leonora Stern, "a majestically large woman," with an ambiguous ethnic background, olive skin, an "imposing" nose, and a "mass of thick black, waving hair, worn shoulder-length and alive with natural oils." She has an amazing dress sense; she goes in for brilliant colors, barbaric-looking amber jewelry, and a yellow silk bandeau (336–37). Her first husband, Nathaniel Stern, was an assistant professor at Princeton (natch), whose timid New Criticism had "totally failed to survive Leonora and the cut-throat ideological battles of structuralism, post-structuralism, Marxism, deconstruction, and feminism" (337). Among her many lovers is the hairy hippy poet, Saul Drucker; an Indian woman professor of anthropology, who introduces her to swooning multiple orgasms; and "Marge, Brigitta, Pocahontas, and Martina" (338).

A newcomer to the fold of academic mystery writers in the '90s was Joanne Dobson, an Americanist at Fordham University. In her series of novels featuring the professor/detective Karen Pelletier, *Quieter Than Sleep* (1997), *The Northbury Papers* (1998), and *The Raven and the Nightingale* (1999), she acknowledges her debt to feminism more readily than Byatt and presents a more optimistic view of the university than her predecessors in the crime genre. A founding editor of the journal *Legacy*, and coeditor along with Judith Fetterley and myself of the Rutgers University series of American Women's Classics, Dobson is an authority on Emily Dickinson and on nineteenth-century American women writers in general. Her sexy, nurturant protagonist Karen Pelletier is the antithesis of the sophisticated Kate Fansler. Pelletier comes from a working-class family in Lowell, Massachusetts, and had to give up a scholarship to Smith when she became pregnant in high school. Divorced from her abusive husband, disowned by her family, she fought her way back to a Ph.D. with help from the Salvation Army, waitressing, night classes, and scholarships.

Now Pelletier is an assistant professor at classy Enfield College in western Massachusetts, recovering from an unhappy love affair with a New York police detective and working on a book on gender and class in the American classics. Enfield was also the name of the Princeton-based college in Carlos Baker's *A Friend in Power*, but here it is a place more like Amherst, although Dobson insists, in an Author's Note reminiscent of Malcolm Bradbury, that "there is no off-ramp on the interstate for Enfield, Massachusetts, no listing for Enfield College occurs in any of the guides to U.S. colleges and universities, and none of Enfield's academic characters has ever paid dues to the MLA."[13]

In all her novels, Dobson gives a wicked picture of the Enfield English department, which has an extraordinarily high homicide rate, the most sexually predatory and unprincipled male faculty members in the world, an unusual number of single parents, abandoned children, and secret affairs, and a large percentage of rich, obnoxious student majors. Like other fictional departments of the '90s, the faculty is split between "the old-guard professors who taught Literature (with a capital L) as high art, and the avant-garde who taught almost anything that had ever appeared in print—and had completely discredited the very idea of art."[14] It includes a flamboyant, publicity-seeking sexuality specialist, Sally Chenille, whose hair changes color weekly; Chenille's book, *Writing on the Body*, "had had a brief notoriety in the media as exemplifying everything that had gone wrong with postmodern intellectual discourse. She'd gotten an NEH grant to write this study of the textual significance of body piercing, tattooing, scarification, and personal branding, and now the Christian Right was up in arms about the debased use of their sacred tax dollars."[15] Enfield English also has faculty members in queer studies, postmodernism, postcolonialism, post-Shakespeare studies, neo-Shakespeare studies, and animality. Randy Astin-Berger, the new Palaver chair, is into Foucault and has a gold stud in his left ear, a melon-colored jacket, and a retro tie. He is simply "a hotshot academic superstar on the make," who teaches "Transgressive American Texts" (215). When he is murdered, it sets "literate tongues wagging" at the MLA.[16]

Overall, however, Dobson writes about feminist scholarship without mocking it. In each book in the series, Pelletier encounters a lost manuscript by an obscure or reviled American woman writer and defends this anticanonical literature against the American classics and against those who would stereotype, diminish, or kill it. In *The Northbury Papers* (1999), for example, so-called sentimental novelist Serena Northbury (partly based on the nineteenth-century writer Mrs. E. D. E. N. Southworth) is presented as the opposite of Melville. Defending Northbury's work, Pelletier says, "She's the only novelist I know from that era who writes about the kind of courage it takes to get through life day by day. No white whales. No uncharted forests. No scarlet letters. No great heroics at all. Just food and drink and perseverance. And ordinary kindness. And ordinary love" (34).

And like Byatt, Dobson writes these lost imaginary texts herself. She invents Northbury's interracial romance, *Child of the North Star*: "Armand circled Emmy with his strong arm, as they looked from the ship's deck back at the receding land of both of their births. She took one final glance at that receding green where the child of her heart slept the long, deep sleep, then turned to her protector, blue eyes gazing deeply into brown" (156). In *The Raven and the Nightingale* (2000), Dobson invents the journals and poems of Emmeline Foster (based on Fanny Osgood and others), rumored to have drowned herself after an unhappy affair with Poe. The poems include "The Bird of the Dream," an influence on "The Raven."

Pelletier is rewarded for her detective efforts by winning for Enfield the gift of a Northbury Center for research on American women writers, a transatlantic version of the feminist archive Maud Bailey runs in *Possession*, and obviously a place with an intellectual mission Dobson fully admires and respects. Unfortunately, it must be located and staffed by Enfield faculty, and so its purposes will be compromised. Like other fictional departments too, the Enfield clan cannot agree on anything. Usually, the department fights over "curriculum reform, course scheduling, and tenure decisions,"[17] and although it is "fond of the appearance of democracy," in reality it is "as hierarchical and class-bound as any medieval fiefdom: Full professors make all the important decisions, associate professors do all the work, assistant professors curtsy whenever the lords of the manor pass by" (131).

Richard Russo's *Straight Man* (1998) further emphasizes the changes between the buoyant and confident midcentury academic life and the pessimisms of the '90s by having its narrator, William Henry Devereaux Jr., be the son of a prominent English professor of an earlier era. Devereaux senior was "an academic opportunist, always in the vanguard of whatever was trendy and chic in literary criticism."[18] In the '50s he was a New Critic; then he became the "Father of American Literary Theory"; finally he wrote a "literary memoir that was short-listed for a major award" (xvii). He preferred to be a visiting professor, with light duties and heavy respect, and to enjoy the perks of a book-lined office and an elegant faculty house.

But his son is a temporary acting chair of English at West Central Pennsylvania University, and he has to preside over anxieties about a rumored purge of tenured faculty that has everyone shaken up. Devereaux is also dragging his feet about the search for a new chair, because "our department is so deeply divided, . . . we have grown so contemptuous of each other over the years, that the sole purpose of bringing in a chair from the outside was to prevent any of us from assuming the reigns [sic] of power. We're looking not so much for a chair as for a blood sacrifice" (17). Devereaux asks his colleague, the chair of foreign languages, how *his* department is doing and gets the reply "Silly, small, mean-spirited, lame. . . . Same as English" (61).

And in the American Midwest, where Malcolm Bradbury had once stepped happily westward, State University of Michigan (SUM, which also stands for "State University of Murder" [40]), has gone the way of other tarnished utopias. Nick Hoffman, the narrator of Lev Raphael's *Death of a Constant Lover* (1999), had once "fallen in love . . . with its spectacular, lush 6,000-acre campus, justly famous for gardens, trees, and landscaping." But "it currently housed close to 50,000 students, or 'customers,' as our idiotic new president liked to say and I suppose we were lucky he hadn't instituted drive-through classes yet."[19] Nick teaches in EAR—English, American Studies, and Rhetoric—and he is facing an up-or-out tenure decision. "SUM was terrified of lawsuits, so administrators rigidly adhered to procedure at all times, and it was officially time for us to get together" (20).

Nick is one of those academics who loves to teach, really *lurves* to teach. As he says, "I had gone into teaching as a double major in English and theater, and being in the classroom did feel like acting. I had a costume—academic drag—a role to play, lines, the potential for great ad-libs, a captive audience, and even better, I was rarely upstaged. The set may have been dreary and predictable, but the performance never was. I felt as intensely alive and concentrated in the classroom as I had onstage" (37). But those days are past. Nick ends, and the century ends, with a lament for paradise lost: "Whenever I'm chatting at conferences with faculty members from other universities, the truth comes out after a drink or two: Hardly any academics are happy where they are, no matter how apt the students, how generous the salary or perks, how beautiful the setting, how light the teaching load, how lavish the research budget. I don't know if it's academia itself that attracts misfits and malcontents, or if the overwhelming hypocrisy of that world would have turned even the Van Trapp family sullen" (180).

The emotional and temporal gulf between Snow's prewar Cambridge, where "men lived the least anxious, the most comforting, the freest lives," and the university at the turn of the century could not be wider. The idyllic ivory tower of *The Masters* has fallen into ruins. Vocation has become employment; critics have become superstars; scholars have become technicians. And not just in the United States, either. In J. M. Coetzee's *Disgrace* (1999), Professor David Lurie

> earns his living at the Cape Technical University, formerly Cape Town University College. Once a professor of modern languages, he has been, since Classics and Modern Languages were closed down as part of the great rationalization, adjunct professor of communications. Like all rationalized personnel, he is allowed to offer one special-field course a year, irrespective of enrolment, because that is good for morale. This year he is offering a course in the Romantic poets. For the rest he teaches Communications 101, "Communication Skills," and Communications 201, "Advanced Communication Skills."[20]

Lurie daydreams about writing a book on Byron, but he knows he will never do it: "He is tired of criticism, tired of prose measured by the yard" (4).

Yet it is not the debasement of the curriculum or the demoralization of the faculty that provide the nuclear plot for the most recent and most pessimistic academic novels, but rather the professors' vulnerability to accusations by students, in an atmosphere dominated by political correctness. Perhaps the credit for pioneering use of the device belongs to David Mamet in his play *Oleanna* (1992), in which a female student destroys an innocent male professor with a false charge of sexual harassment. Coetzee picked up on the theme in *Disgrace*, which won the Booker Prize, and Coetzee has since won the Nobel Prize in Literature, and in the new century other very distinguished novelists took up the cry. Coetzee's alienated Professor Lurie has an affair with a student, Melanie Isaacs, and she lodges a complaint for sexual harassment. The university committee on discipline calls him in, and rather than defend himself, he pleads guilty but refuses to apologize, to accept counseling, or to acknowledge any penalty. "Repentance is neither here nor there," he tells the committee. "Repentance belongs to another world, to another universe of discourse" (58). He resigns his job, much to the relief of his department chair, a chilly spinster named Elaine Winter.

But later he visits the girl's parents and speaks to her father: "In my own terms, I am being punished for what happened between myself and your daughter. I am sunk into a state of disgrace from which it will not be easy to lift myself. It is not a punishment I have refused. . . . On the contrary, I am . . . trying to accept disgrace as my state of being" (172). Lurie starts to write an opera called *Byron in Italy*, "a chamber-play about love and death, with a passionate young woman and a once passionate but now less than passionate older man" (180). It is that loss of passion that seems to obsess the novelists, and no doubt Mamet too. Although *Oleanna* clearly shows that nothing happened, Mamet can hardly have thought false charges were the real problem, for in an interview he said candidly, "When I was single and teaching twenty years ago, I didn't know a professor who wasn't having an affair with a student."[21] The climactic moment in the play arrives when the mild-mannered professor is finally provoked to violence. To many authors looking at the university around 2000, it seemed that the risks and the joys of the erotics of teaching had succumbed to an increasingly bureaucratic and soulless institutionalization.

chapter 6

∿

Into the Twenty-First Century

TRAGIC TOWERS

IN AN ESSAY IN the *New York Times* in October 2000, the cultural critic Sarah Boxer observed that the academic novel seemed suddenly bleaker: "This year the American campus novel has staked out rougher territory, something more tragic. . . . What has changed? What has made these later works darker? Is it bitterness about deconstruction and the death of the author? Is it AIDS? Is it a backlash against feminism? Against youth?"[1] The darkly apocalyptic tone of the fiction of the new century had been set in the '90s, a pattern we have seen in previous decades; but as major novelists, including Francine Prose, Philip Roth, and Saul Bellow, began to use the genre of academic fiction, it became more visible and took on literary gravitas and grandeur. While earlier academic novels had been idyllic, satiric, ironic, or even embittered, these were cosmic, mythic, and vengeful.

The dominant plot of the *Professorroman* in the first years of the first decade of the century was sexual harassment. The randy professor had appeared in various forms before, especially in Malcolm Bradbury's *The History Man*. But as we saw in the last chapter, in the late 1990s, sex took over, as writers well outside the academic fold, like Coetzee and Mamet, used themes of harassment to explore academic hypocrisy, morality, and puritanism. Oddly, fictional professors do not imitate their real brethren in one crucial detail: seeking legal counsel. Perhaps this is merely a literary strategy; nothing is duller than the nitpicking procedural wrangles that occupy most of the time in most judicial hearings, probably more so in universities than in real courtrooms. When Coetzee has Professor Lurie decline to defend himself, he can move on quickly to the next stage, the fall from grace that is the novel's theme. Writers and their protagonists no longer recognize the university's moral authority to solve its problems and resolves its quarrels intramurally. The professor in the throes of a midlife crisis, realizing that he will never write his great book, that he has lost touch with his field, that he no longer reaches his students, and often that his personal life is just as hollow, is actually an emblem of the academic institution as a whole. It, too, cannot fulfill its academic mission and cannot govern itself.

In *Blue Angel* (2000), Francine Prose retells the story of the classic film about a dignified professor whose infatuation with a nightclub performer leads to his degradation. In this version, however, we are not in Berlin but in Euston College in rural Vermont. The central figure, Theodore "Ted" Swenson, is a forty-seven-year-old creative writing teacher who is suffering from a years-long writer's block; furthermore, his college-age daughter Ruby is no longer speaking to him, and his marriage to Sherrie, who works in the college clinic, has gone a bit stale. The object of Swenson's passion is not a Marlene Dietrich playing Lola Lola, but one of his students, Angela Argo, a "skinny, pale redhead with neon-orange and lime-green streaks in her hair and a delicate, sharp-featured face pierced in a half-dozen places," wearing "an arsenal of chains, dog collars, and bracelets."[2] Unlike his other students, Angela has real talent as a writer, and Swenson's efforts to help her prove to be his undoing.

Blue Angel is told entirely through Swenson's perspective, so that parts of the story remain mysterious. Most readers take it as another satire on political correctness, a new puritanism run amok. There is a lot to support that reading. The novel begins by invoking a case at nearby State (where Ruby goes), in which a professor of art history has been suspended for saying "Yum!" when he showed a slide of a Greek sculpture of a female nude (18). Euston's dean calls a meeting to remind his own faculty of the sexual harassment policy, in a chapel with a portrait of Jonathan Edwards, and Swenson regards the event and the policy as a "symptom of their hangover from Puritan repression" (21). In the chapel and at a later dinner party, Swenson's colleagues are portrayed pretty much as the usual suspects, a man-hating feminist, a gay theorist, a smooth-talking insincere dean, and so on.

Swenson, however, is no hero. He is not writing anymore himself, and he does not teach much either, a fact that comes out indirectly at his hearing: "Amelia and Bill shoot looks at Swenson. His teaching load *has* been light" (297). He is what frustrated deans call deadwood. Furthermore, he regularly alienates his friends, from his wife's coworker Arlene to his own colleague and fellow writer Magda to his New York agent Len, whom he accuses of child abuse, inadvertently, but even he knows that is no excuse. As he reflects after his snipe at Arlene, "Speech pops out of him, on its own" (19). One reason is that he is an alcoholic, although he does not seem to be aware of it. At the dean's party, he gets drunk and proposes that they try desensitizing the "whiners bitching about sexual harassment. Lock them in a room and shout dirty words at them until they grow up. Shit shit shit. Fuck fuck fuck" (107). Once the scandal of his affair with Angela breaks, he withdraws into his house and drinks alone until the hearing, not even bothering to prepare a defense or ask whether he can have a lawyer. He confesses his affair to Sherrie only when he knows that the secret is out, staging the scene clumsily in a restaurant, and she reveals a completely new version of his performance as a father, calling him "a guy whose own daughter won't talk to him because he forgot she existed, he was so self-involved, so in love with his own problems, so interested in his own little ideas about this or that meaningless bullshit, so the only way she can get his attention is to start going out with a guy whose reputation is so bad even her father will have heard about it, even with his head so far up his ass. . . . So you got a replacement daughter" (254). Finally, of course, unlike Mamet's hapless professor, Swenson had sex with Angela, not fully consummated only because he broke a tooth and lost his erection.

So Swenson is no standard-bearer for common sense or decency, even though he wins a certain amount of sympathy just by telling his own tale. But Angela is no victim either. She leads him on at every step, seeks him out, asks him for help, writes about a student with a crush on her professor. Magda warns him that Angela is trouble, including the unfortunately irresistible information that she wrote a collection of erotic poems in the persona of a phone sex worker. At the end, her actions reveal a sinister side: she had gone to the college clinic, claiming to be suicidal, where Sherrie, in talking her through her depression, had told her the story of how she and Swenson met, a story Angela then put into her own manuscript for Swenson's class. Angela also turns out to be a friend of Ruby's disreputable ex-boyfriend, who shows up at the hearing to testify that Ruby told him she had been molested by her father. Angela pressures Swenson into taking her manuscript to his agent (who, ironically, likes it and gets her a publishing deal), then tells him that "the only reason I let you fuck me was so you would help me get this novel to someone who could do something" (236), and ultimately tells the hearing that Swenson proposed the idea to her. And finally she secretly tapes the conversation with her unlucky professor, in which he admits having sex with her.

Francine Prose never lets us know the truth about Angela. There is no answer to Swenson's desperate final outburst to Angela after the hearing, "Just tell me one thing, okay? What the fuck were you doing?" (312). Understandably, Swenson wonders if there has been a giant conspiracy against him, but it would be hard to make a plausible argument for that interpretation. Rather, *Blue Angel* is the self-portrait of a man coming undone through his own faults, products of a lifetime of self-indulgence and egocentric irresponsibility. His punishment seems cruel only because the avenging Angela and the disciplinary committee are no better than he is. At the end, Swenson feels liberated by his disgrace, like Coetzee's Lurie. He hears the college bells chime and imagines that they toll for him, "announcing the triumph over another male oppressor, one small step along the path toward a glorious future. He's glad to be out of that future and headed into his own" (314).

This refusal of university "justice" and this existential suffering, of which sexual harassment is the symptom, also lies at the heart of Philip Roth's *The Human Stain* (2000). Coleman Silk, a classics professor and former dean of the faculty at Athena, loses his job because of a mistaken accusation. Inquiring after two students who have never come to class, Silk asks whether they are "spooks"; they turn out to be black, and they bring suit for racial abuse and discrimination. He refuses to apologize or admit guilt: "The charge of racism is spurious. It is preposterous . . . the charge is not just false—it is spectacularly false."[3] But in the stress of the ensuing brouhaha, his wife Iris has a stroke and dies; in outrage, he resigns from the college. It's a drastic step, because had he retired "in his own good time, there would have been the festschrift, there would have been the institution of the Coleman Silk Lecture Series, there would have been a classical studies chair established in his name. . . . In the small academic world where he had lived the bulk of his life, he would have long ceased to be resented or controversial, or even feared, and, instead, officially glorified forever" (6).

So Coleman's Silk's defiance is a "No in Thunder," a heroic act of civil disobedience in the face of political correctness. And then Roth comes up with a shocker: Silk is actually black himself, passing as white and Jewish. In the aftermath of his retirement from Athena, he decides to abandon the life of the mind for the ecstasy of the body and begins a much-gossiped-about affair with Faunia Farley, a janitor at the college thirty years his junior. Roth sets the novel in the political framework of the summer of 1998—the summer of Bill Clinton, Monica Lewinsky, and the infamous stain—and uses this as the context for the sexual politics of the novel: "It was the summer when—for the billionth time—the jumble, the mayhem, the mess proved itself more subtle than this one's ideology and that one's morality. It was the summer when a president's penis was on everyone's mind, and life, in all its shameless impurity, once again confounded America" (3).

Unlike Coetzee's David Lurie, Silk is unrepentant, glorying in this late love; and unlike Prose's Ted Swenson, he is a revered figure, a great scholar, a forceful teacher, and an effective administrator. He does not feel disgraced by his sexuality, only enraged at the academic community's snobbery and timidity. Taking Viagra to enable his sexual relationship with Faunia, the aging Silk compares himself to Zeus: "I've come to understand Zeus's amorous transformations" (32). The secret of his real parentage comes out only through the detective work of the novel's narrator, Nathan Zuckerman, that same Zuckerman who had gone to seek out E. I. Lonoff at Athena (or Athene, as it was called then) College in the 1970s and is now living there as a recluse himself.

Roth also employs the framework of classical myth and tragedy to illuminate Silk's career. Silk teaches a course called GHM—Gods, Heroes, and Myth—and he lectures at the first class meeting on *The Iliad* and Achilles, "who, through the strength of his rage at an insult—the insult of not getting the girl—isolates himself, positions himself defiantly outside the very society whose glorious protector he is and whose need of him is enormous. . . . In this offense against the phallic entitlement, the phallic *dignity*, of a powerhouse of a warrior prince, is how the great imaginative literature of Europe begins" (5). He is a man who studies anger in classical literature and knows, "from the wrath of Achilles, the rage of Philoctetes, the fulminations of Medea, the madness of Ajax, the despair of Electra, and the suffering of Prometheus, the many horrors that can ensue when the highest degree of indignation is achieved, and in, the name of justice, retribution is exacted, and a cycle of retaliation begins" (63). Silk's fate is the matter of classical tragedy, with desire as the human stain on the silk fabric and rage as the rent in the cloth, although he resolves "to live in a way that does not bring Philoctetes to mind" (170).

Seen through the eyes of Nathan Zuckerman, Silk's administrative career was abrasive and ruthless. "As dean, and with the full support of an ambitious new president, Coleman had taken an antiquated, backwater, Sleepy Hollowish college, and, not without steamrolling, put an end to the place as a gentlemen's farm by aggressively encouraging the deadwood among the faculty's old guard to seek early retirement, recruiting ambitious young assistant professors, and revolutionizing the curriculum" (5). Silk summons the faculty to his office to discuss their C.V.s, and ask what they have been doing with their time. He abolishes the local quarterly in which they have been publishing oddments of their dissertations; he makes them apply formally for sabbatical, eat in the student cafeteria, show up for faculty meetings, and teach freshman composition.

Silk's major faculty antagonist, however, is not a demoted and humiliated Old Boy but a young feminist professor of French, Delphine Roux, the chair of Languages and Literature. She has been a leader of the faculty group protesting his "racist" comments. When she finds out that he is having an affair with Faunia, she sends him an anonymous poison-pen letter:

Everyone knows you're
sexually exploiting an
abused, illiterate
woman half your
age. (38)

Delphine is the antithesis of Faunia Farley. She is a French intellectual striver, who has attended the best schools—Lycée Henri IV, École Normal Supérieure de Fontenay, Yale. She sounds a lot like Julia Kristeva, who has written about an America Jewish novelist resembling Philip Roth in her novel *The Samurai*. At one point, Roux is actually reading "a book by Julia Kristeva, a treatise as wonderful as any ever written on melancholy" and sees a man reading something by Kristeva's husband, Philippe Sollers (200). Coleman disdains her: "To Coleman she embodied the sort of prestigious academic crap that the Athena students needed like a hole in the head but whose appeal to the faculty second-raters would prove irresistible" (190). In the academic fiction of the '90s, a feminist faculty member often plays the role of the sexually frustrated spinster, the prude who cannot understand the man's Dionysian drive.

Delphine is a beautiful young woman, but Roth would have us believe that she too is overwhelmed by desire for Coleman Silk. Lonely and secretly attracted to Coleman, she sees his affair with Faunia as a masked revenge on her: "Faunia Farley was his substitute for her. Through Faunia Farley he was striking back at her. Who else's face and name and form does she suggest to you but mine—the mirror image of me" (195). As a feminist, she rationalizes this jealousy and resentment by telling herself that "her whole life had been a battle not to be cowed by the Coleman Silks, who use their privilege to overpower everyone else and do exactly as they please" (197). Moreover, Delphine does not like other feminists either. At Athena, to her distress, "there is a cabal of three women—a philosophy professor, a sociology professor, and a history professor—who particularly drive her crazy. Full of animosity toward her simply because she is not ploddingly plugged in the way they are. Because she has an air of chic, they feel she hasn't read enough learned journals" (271). Delphine calls them "Les Trois Grasses"—not the Three Graces but "The Three Greaseballs" (272). She fakes an elaborate scenario of revenge against Silk and against these women by claiming to have been harassed by Coleman herself.

Whereas Coetzee's and Prose's professors live on with a new and bitter wisdom, Silk dies in an apparent accident, which is actually the revenge of Faunia's ex-husband, an insanely angry Vietnam veteran. For Zuckerman and for Roth, this death is tragic, the fall of a hero who had won great victories, only to become ensared in petty affairs. Roth also connects Athena to the grand sweep of history. What happens to Coleman Silk is an echo of what happened to President Clinton. Coleman Silk himself is a product of history, rising out of the black ghettoes of the segregated postwar 1940s. Faunia's ex-husband is a casualty of American hubris in Vietnam. The moral failure of Athena is the shame of our whole society.

Aggression toward women, exploitation by women, and its psychological roots, are also the subject of James Lasdun's *The Horned Man* (2002). Lawrence Miller is a British professor of gender studies who sits on the Sexual Harassment Committee at Arthur Clay College in New York. His antagonist on the committee is the school attorney, a sexually frustrated middle-aged woman named Elaine Jordan (a disconcerting number of strange and unpleasant women in academic novels are named Elaine), who also seems oddly attracted to him. He is separated from his wife, hostile toward most of his colleagues, but anxious to succeed. He is also concealing a traumatic childhood, gets terrible migraine headaches, and sees a female psychotherapist.

As in Malamud's *A New Life*, Lasdun uses the figure of the academic double to represent Miller's repressed wishes. Miller is using the haunted office of a dead professor, Barbara Hellermann, who seems to have been murdered in a tenured position. He also hears about a legendary bad professor, Bogomil Trumilcik, a visiting poet from "Romania or Bulgaria or one of those places," who has disappeared. Trumilcik was a tomcat: "He made passes at practically every female he taught. Then when someone finally complained about him to the President, instead of being embarrassed, he went totally crazy. He made this terrible commotion right out there on campus. . . . Finally he ran off down Mulberry Street, screaming and yelling like a madman."[4]

Trumilcik shows up frequently throughout the novel, as the director of a play based on Kafka's short story "Blumfield," as a writer, and as a possible serial killer. At the same time, Miller seems to be stalking his ex-wife, an art historian and medievalist. When he traces her to The Cloisters, where she is curating an exhibit on unicorns, he hallucinates that he has become a unicorn himself, a phallic monster. In this dizzying postmodern tale, Lasdun explores both male sexual violence and its theorized academic forms and also protests against the female-dominated political correctness of the university. At one point, the students stage a rally in favor of sexual harassment: "Give us the freedom to fuck who we choose!" (167). Lasdun ends with a vision of Miller in hiding, contemplating the Gnostic gospels and their message of self-expression: "If you bring forth what is within you, what you bring forth will save you. If you do not bring forth what is within you, what you do not bring forth will destroy you" (195).

Like Lasdun, James Hynes is a brilliant rewriter, inventor of literary texts, and admirer of the supernatural and occult as well as the gothic. In his hilarious, hard-hitting *The Lecturer's Tale* (2001), a lowly lecturer, Nelson Humboldt, makes his way through the English department of the University of the Midwest in Hamilton Groves, Minnesota.[5] Humboldt is an academic outsider in the land of the postmodern; his father was an embittered, ABD high-school teacher who raised him on bedtime stories from the literary canon—"Beowulf in the bassinet, Piers Plowman in the crib" (14)—so that he has "an unusually thorough memory" of it (6). His college mentor loans him books by Trilling and teaches him prosody, so that by the time he gets to graduate school, among multiculturalists and theorists, his first lesson "was to keep his mouth shut" (21). Eventually Nelson tries to conform to academic fashion; he had wanted to write his dissertation on "Guilt and Predestination in the Works of James Hogg, 1770–1835" (25) but had been persuaded by the trendy to write on Conrad and postcolonialism instead. Then he grinds out "Hogg article after Hogg article, ending up with a book-length manuscript of unpublished and mutually exclusive chapters, each of which proved with equal conviction that James Hogg was a virgin and a libertine; a misogynist and an early feminist; hegemonic and transgressive; imperialist and postcolonial; patriarchal and matriarchal; straight, bisexual, and queer" (33). Finally he writes "The Transgendered Calvinist: James Hogg in Butlerian Perspective" (33) and gives up scholarship in despair.

The department dismisses Nelson from his tenuous position as adjunct visiting lecturer, threatens to throw him out of university housing, and undermines his ability to support his wife and children; most of the novel is about his revenge. In a bicycle accident near the campus, Nelson's right index finger is severed, and when it is sewn back on in the university hospital, it proves to have magical powers that enable him to make those he touches do his bidding. He uses this supernatural power to win back his job and also to attempt to get tenure for his one departmental ally and friend, Vita Deonne, a wan gender theorist who works on the lesbian phallus in literature. Vita, whose name not only alludes to Virgina Woolf's lover Vita Sackville-West, the inspiration for Orlando, but also suggests the curriculum vitae of the academic is a person whose work is truly her life, as Nelson comes to understand.

Moreover, Nelson wants to overthrow the unjust English department structure, in which the rich and powerful have offices and secretaries at the top of the tower, and the composition program is housed in the shabby basement and composed of pale women, "the Morlocks of the Eloi world," or perhaps the bloodless female mill workers in Melville's short story "The Tartarus of Maids," or the mythic denizens of Hades, ruled over by program director Linda Proserpina. To Nelson, the place feels like a sweatshop: "In each cubicle a thin woman in thrift shop couture sat earnestly tutoring some groggy student . . . most of the comp teachers were divorced moms and single women with cats who taught eight classes a year and earned a thousand dollars per class. . . . They were the steerage of the English Department, the first to drown if the budget sprang a leak" (63).

On the eighth floor of the tower is the office of the department chairman, Anthony Pescecane, an Italian-American native of Hoboken who wrote a celebrated dissertation on *Paradise Lost* called "To Reign in Hell" and a book called "Screw Free Speech" (79–80). The power-mad Pescecane has been quoted as saying "that the finest thing in life is to take an academic department and bend it to one's will" (93). MLA members may see hints here of yet another incarnation of Stanley Fish and an allusion to his 1967 book on Milton, *Surprised by Sin*; but one reviewer, to my delight, described Pescecane as "the evil spawn of Elaine Showalter and Tony Soprano."[6]

Playing Caliban to Pescecane's Prospero is the stumpy administrative assistant Lionel Grossmaul, a once-brilliant theorist reduced by writer's block to "following his grad school friend from triumph to triumph in a series of dead-end administrative jobs" (97). Among the full professors, the department also includes a traditional Cleanth-Brooks-clone named Morton Weissman (i.e., dead white man); the predatory Miranda DeLaTour; the sex theorist Penelope O., who says "my sexual preference is undergraduate" (165); the professionally Irish poet Timothy Coogan; the undergraduate chair Victoria Victorinx, who is famous for her theory of clitoral hegemony; and the anarchic Marko Kraljevic and his lover Lorraine Alsace. The usual suspects, again, and one of these people is sending the others poison-pen letters, a collage of quotations from Pound, Eliot, Joyce, Wilde, and Brontë.

On one level, *The Lecturer's Tale* is about the revenge of literature on theory. The novel begins with an epigraph from "The Pardoner's Tale" and ends with a close parody of Chaucer's "Retraction," or afterword to *The Canterbury Tales*. The English department's structure is taken from *The Tempest* and *Paradise Lost*; the faculty come out of the Gothic novel, Bloomsbury legend, and gender theory. From the first sentence, as the library clock strikes thirteen as in *1984*, to the last sentence, which echoes *David Copperfield*, Hynes has managed to get in apt, surprising, and clever references to a huge range of canonical writers, critics, and texts, with chapter titles like "Nelson in Nighttown," "Discipline and Punish," and "The Story of O," and sly allusions to everyone from Catherine MacKinnon to Borges. In short, *The Lecturer's Tale* is a Norton Anthology of a novel, a course in a book, that covers all the literary material of an introductory survey in English literature.

In particular, though, Hynes goes for the epic and the satanic; the university coffee shop is called Pandemonium, and Milton's Hell is not far from his image of the modern university department of literature. As Nelson, armed with his magical finger, struggles against all these figures and forces, the novel becomes increasingly literary, apocalyptic, and carnivalesque, an explosion of masques, infernos, labyrinths, shape-shifters, ghosts, spirits, and conspirators. Eventually Nelson has to face his own complicity in the gender politics of the university and to realize that he himself is the Dead White Male haunting the library, the mad adjunct in the Poole Annex.

But the novel has a surprisingly positive and even utopian ending. His revenge complete, his job restored, his victory assured, Nelson plans a new English department on the ruins of the old one. It will be "a department that rises above petty politics, that melds the best of both worlds" of traditional scholarship and cutting-edge theory, teaching and research (369). Even Chairman Pescecane renounces literary theory in a "high-profile article in *The New York Times Magazine*" and commits himself "for the rest of his life to teaching undergraduates and only undergraduates, to love the same great, canonical works of literature that had rescued him from the docklands of New Jersey" (380). The book ends with Nelson preparing to teach his class and wondering if reading novels can make any difference at all in people's lives. "Would *The Great Gatsby* raise their pay? Would *Wuthering Heights* lighten the burden of a dead end job?" (385–86). Never to know, he decides, is both the enigma of teaching literature and its glory.

Novels in which male professors are seduced and not just abandoned but denounced and destroyed by female students have fared very well with the critics. Jonathan Franzen won a National Book Award for *The Corrections* (2001), in which Chip Lambert plays the fall guy. He teaches at D—— College, somewhere in Connecticut, with "an elite reputation and a middling endowment"; like the other untenured faculty, he lives "in semi-squalor . . . in a damp cinderblock development" with a patio overlooking a stream known to the locals as Carparts Creek.[7] But Chip is one of the lucky ones; he partners the provost at doubles in tennis and helps him win a long-coveted faculty championship, and as a result he is "all but guaranteed lifelong employment" (33). A member of the department of Textual Artifacts (reminiscent of DeLillo's department of American Environments), he teaches a trendy course called "Consuming Narratives," devoted to demystifying American advertising (DeLillo's Prof. Siskind teaches "American Icons"). Like Lasdun's Lawrence Miller, Chip Lambert is ostensibly one of the new breed of feminist-friendly males; he had "co-chaired the committee that drafted the college's stringent new policy on faculty-student contacts" (37). So he is sure he can handle the situation when Melissa Paquette starts pursuing him, galloping after him to turn in a paper, standing too close to him at a reception, materializing in a parking lot to help clear snow from his car, leaving him roses on Valentine's Day and chocolate on Easter, and finally vandalizing his screen door.

The scene where Melissa retaliates for Chip's rebuffs is a brilliant

and gratifying comic classroom drama. The day's topic is the W——
Corporation's recent ad campaign called "You Go, Girl!" In a
sequence of vignettes, a woman reveals that she has breast cancer, is
put in touch with up-to-date information and a support network
through W——'s technology, but in the "campaign's revolutionary
inspiration" (39) she succumbs to the disease, and the final install-
ment is a tearjerking pitch to "Help Us Fight for the Cure" (40).
Chip wants the class to say that the ads are cynical and manipulative,
but the students think they are brave and really interesting, "good
for the culture and good for the country" (41). Chip's last hope is
Melissa, who he thinks has grasped the point of his course and is not
just "parroting the weekly jargon" (42). Melissa, however, turns on
him, says that he cares about their opinions only when they agree
with him, delivers a cogent defense of the "You Go, Girl!" campaign,
and when Chip tries to hide behind Baudrillard, she bursts out:

> This whole class, it's just bullshit every week. It's one critic after
> another wringing their hands about the state of criticism. Nobody can
> ever quite say what's wrong exactly. But they all know it's evil. They
> all know "corporate" is a dirty word. And if somebody's having fun or
> getting rich—disgusting! Evil! And it's always the death of this and the
> death of that. And people who think they're free aren't "really" free.
> And people who think they're happy aren't "really" happy. . . . Here
> things are getting better and better for women and people of color,
> and gay men and lesbians, more and more integrated and open, and
> all you can think about is some stupid, lame problem with signifiers
> and signifieds. Like, the only way you can make something bad out of
> an ad that's great for women—which you have to do, because there
> has to be something wrong with everything—is to say it's evil to be
> rich and evil to work for a corporation. (44)

You go, girl!

The next semester, everything comes apart for Chip. His rival for
promotion, a feminist theorist named Vendla O'Fallon, publishes a
memoir called *Daddy's Girl,* which is glowingly reviewed in the *New
York Times Book Review* (52–53). Then his mentor, the tennis-loving
provost, has a stroke. A few days later, the demoralized Chip has sex

with Melissa, and over Thanksgiving recess they go off together, stopping at a motel well short of their intended destination, where they engage in uninterrupted, chemically enhanced sex for a week. Needless to say, Melissa reports a damning version of all this to the college, and Chip is invited to resign by the acting provost, Cali Lopez, a Filipina lesbian who had been denied tenure a few years before for "having claimed to have a degree she didn't have," but was retained and promoted after protests (83).

Typically, Chip mounts no effective defense and uses "the last $220 of credit on his Visa card to buy eight bottles of a rather tasty Fronsac" (83). He makes a bit more of an effort than some of his fictional peers by borrowing ten thousand dollars from his sister to hire a lawyer to "sue D—— College for wrongful termination of his contract. This was a waste of money, but it felt good" (87). Then he moves to New York and conceives "revenge in the form of a screen-play that would expose the narcissism and treachery of Melissa Paquette and the hypocrisy of his colleagues" (87). Chip labors for months on this script, called *The Academy Purple*, a delicious mock-ery of academic writing, in which "Bill Quaintence, an attractive young professor of Textual Artifacts, is seduced by his beautiful and adoring student Mona," only to have his happiness wrecked by his estranged wife Hillaire, who seduces Mona with "crypto-repressive rhetoric" in a "clash of Therapeutic and Transgressive worldviews" (26–27). Realizing that the story has problems, "to salvage his artis-tic and intellectual ambitions, he added a long theoretical opening monologue," which becomes the whole focus of his revisions as he tries to shorten it, "all the while struggling to believe that stars and producers in Prada jackets would enjoy reading six pages (but not seven) of turgid academic theorizing" (91). If Chip were a better writer, *The Academy Purple* could be *Oleanna*, or *Blue Angel*, or even *The Corrections*. Or as Chip the critic might have put it, Franzen stages the scene of writing in a classic *mise en abîme*.

Finally, having maxed out all his credit cards and exhausted even his sister's generosity, Chip is forced to sell his academic library. "He purged the Marxists from his bookshelves and took them to the Strand in two extremely heavy bags. The books were in their origi-nal jackets and had an aggregate list price of $3,900. A buyer at the

Strand appraised them casually and delivered his verdict: 'Sixty-five'"
(92). Three months later, he has "sold his feminists, his formalists,
his structuralists, his poststructuralists, his Freudians, and his queers"
(93). All he had left were "his beloved cultural historians and his
complete hardcover Arden Shakespeare" so "he piled his Foucault
and Greenblatt and hooks and Poovey into shopping bags and sold
them all for $115" (93). It's a funny reprise of a classic fictional scene,
where emblems of a treasured past, objects laden with nostalgic emotions, historical meaning, and sentimental value are sold to unfeeling
strangers, reduced to their commercial price and status as inert plain
things.

Up to this point in *The Corrections*, despite some great original
riffs, Franzen has followed the standard formula for academic novels
of sexual harassment: a hapless male professor is entrapped by a predatory and deceitful girl with no obvious motive and faces a rigged
system of judgment controlled by a network of militantly hostile
women. At this point in *The Corrections*, about one-sixth of the way
through, Franzen abruptly leaves the academic novel and turns his
attention elsewhere. Like other nonacademic novelists working in
the genre, he has larger ambitions. Franzen's title is a multiple pun;
all kinds of "corrections" appear in the work, from Chip's correction of student papers to the penal house of correction to a cook's
correction of a sauce to corrections in the stock market. Those deval-
ued books of literary theory represent a market correction in the academic world. Chip has been peddling his ideas successfully, but he
has been relying on the "greater fool" model, assisted by fresh supplies of naive students each year. It's a "Ponzi" scheme, a pyramid or
bubble, and once the supply of suckers runs out, or they wise up and
stop buying, the market collapses.

The Corrections is a long and complex novel, which tells the life
stories of Chip's entire family—his brother Gary, a prospering money
manager; his sister Denise, a talented chef; his father Alfred, a retired
railroad worker with Parkinson's disease and dementia; and his
mother Enid, an anxious fussbudget of a homemaker. All the characters seem comic at first, but reveal moving and even tragic human
depths by the end. The climax of the novel is a Christmas reunion
of the family, and all the characters emerge from the experience

changed, their understanding of their lives "corrected," so to speak. Chip is no different from the others. He has spent most of the novel in Lithuania, helping an amiable conman defraud foreign investors, and he barely escapes with his life when political chaos descends on the little country. As he makes his chastened way across the border to Poland, he has an epiphany about his old screenplay: "The tragic Bill Quaintence became a comic fool" (537). Franzen is kind to Chip Lambert; the errant professor makes it home for the holiday, he is reconciled with his family, his sister forgives his debts to her, and he even meets and marries a doctor and becomes the father of twins. And he continues to revise his screenplay, while working occasionally as a substitute teacher.

With *The Corrections*, the university fully merges with the rest of society. It is not a special institution, as it was to Snow and as it seemed to many other academic novelists that it might once have been or might yet become. In Franzen's world, academia is only one of many quirky institutions, comparable to Wall Street, haute cuisine, medicine, big business, cruise liners, or families. In all of them, individuals are flawed and deluded but capable of heroism and love. With luck, even a professor may find the honesty, humility, and compassion to discover that truth and to see his own role in proper perspective. But he probably won't get to do it while on the job.

Saul Bellow's *Ravelstein* (2000) barely qualifies as a novel.[8] Abe Ravelstein is an acknowledged portrait of Bellow's friend, the political philosopher and University of Chicago professor Alan Bloom, and Bellow himself appears in this plotless memoir under the name Chick. Most of the anecdotes and incidents follow reality pretty closely. Ravelstein dies of HIV complications, as Bloom himself did in 1992. Chick almost dies from having eaten a poisonous fish while on vacation in the Caribbean, just like Bellow. Ravelstein gets rich from a cantankerous polemical book on American education, which Chick urges him to write. The book was called *The Closing of the American Mind*; Bloom published it in 1987 with a preface by Bellow, and it became a huge best-seller. It is rather surprising that Bellow's novel in effect outed Bloom as a homosexual; despite all the publicity around his book, this aspect of his life had remained private, and many of his mainly right-wing fans would have been dismayed to learn of it.

Political correctness, sexual harassment, and the other standard themes of academic novels do not appear in *Ravelstein*, except incidentally. The eponymous hero shares, in fact, the despairing vision of many of the writers we have discussed; according to Chick, Ravelstein argued that "while you could get an excellent technical training in the U.S., liberal education had shrunk to the vanishing point" (47). As anyone who has read Bloom knows, he was an unabashed elitist, and unlike most of the fictional protagonists, "he returned to the University as a full professor after two decades on lesser campuses" (61)—that is, to a position where he could do very much as he pleased. He teaches only graduate students, and "when students didn't meet his standards, he said, 'I was wrong about you. This is no place for you. I won't have you around.' The feelings of the rejects didn't concern him" (42). For a time, all he lacked was the money to live in the high style, and his successful book takes care of that; he can stay at the Crillon like Michael Jackson, dribble coffee on his $4,500 Lanvin gold flannel jacket, and buy a custom-fitted BMW for his Filipino companion. Eat your heart out, Morris Zapp!

Bellow was writing an elegiac tribute to a friend, not a satirical novel. Although most critics praised the work, it did not convey to me any of Bloom's alleged charisma and charm. *Ravelstein*'s merits are rather in its extended meditation on two themes, mortality and Jewishness. In both areas, it extends and enriches the tradition that Roth in particular had already worked so fruitfully. For both Roth and Bellow, the university is really an incidental setting; they examine the same themes in many aspects of American life. Chick, the fictional Bellow, is not a professor himself, only a man who has lived near a great university and associated with professors, as the real Bellow had done. In many ways, *Ravelstein* brings the course of the academic novel back to where it started, with some changes that reflect the historical evolution. Bellow esteems the university, the old-fashioned university that is disappearing, because it shelters eccentrics of genius like Bloom. It is a place where one can live the life of the mind, like C. P. Snow's Cambridge. It is nevertheless a large leap from there to Bellow's Chicago, where the grand tradition now embraces all races, all faiths, both sexes, and all sexual orientations. In my mind, Ravelstein embodies a contradiction between the inclusiveness he benefits from and the conservative exclusivity he preaches. For my own part, I would far rather be on the faculty in Athena, Euston, Enfield, College-on-the-Hill, Watermouth, Rummidge, Euphoria, or any of the other campuses imagined by the satirists, arguing with the politically correct ideologues, laughing at my colleagues' follies, and groaning at the students' mistakes, than discussing Plato and Hegel with Chick and Ravelstein.

Conclusion

OVER THE PAST fifty years, the *Professorroman* has offered a full social history of the university, as well as a spiritual, political, and psychological guide to the profession. Each decade has foregrounded the scandal and headlines of higher education—class, political infighting, feminism, sexual harassment, political correctness. How has it changed?

In the '50s and '60s, the academic novel was basically Trollopian. The university was a small, enclosed place, but related to the larger society, affected by its values and problems, and even a model of its ideal state. The academic novel in midcentury confidently presented its dilemmas as microcosms; its political ethics, election campaigns, divisions between the humanities and the sciences, individual tensions between the private and public life, between humble vocation and self-promotion were not imagined as little squabbles but ways of dealing with larger social issues within a manageable scale. Like the disputes between the Broad and the High Church over doctrine and behavior, the internal quarrels of the professors over methods and ideas seemed genuine, if overintense. By and large, even the least attractive inhabitants of academia—Winslow and Nightingale in *The Masters*, Professor Welch and Margaret Peel in *Lucky Jim*, Henry Mulcahy in *The Groves of Academe*, Buchanan in *The Party at Cranton*—were more pathetic and absurd than sinister. And the most admired characters—Lewis Elliot, Domna Rejnev, Edward Tyler, Sandy Sanderling—believed in the work they did and strove to live up to its ideals.

But by the 1970s, this picture of the academic life began to darken and change. Paradoxically, as higher education became larger, taking in more and more students from different backgrounds and classes, meeting the economic demand for highly trained workers and the social need for upward mobility, the old-fashioned professor became as obsolete as the Victorian clergyman, and the new generation of academics, motivated less by faith and service than by ambition and the longing for power, took over fiction. Their fads and squabbles look increasingly petty; they become more and more grotesque figures, full of self-doubt and self-hatred. By the time we get to the novels of sexual harassment, the conflicts—over sexuality and race—could be said to be central and profound, but the academic novelists satirize the way the university community deals with them as quirky, pedantic, vengeful, legalistic, and inhumane. The ivory towers have become fragile fortresses with glassy walls.

When I started reading academic novels, I was a naive student with very little hope of entering the world of the masters, and no expectation, let alone ambition, of succeeding in it. Now that I have come to the other side of that dream and that career, to the fifth season of the academic calendar, retirement, how much did I learn from my decades of reading academic novels? How useful a guide are they to the real life of a professor, or at least to the more-or-less real life I lived as a professor myself?

Overall, I think, contemporary academic fiction is too tame, substituting satire for tragedy, detective plots for the complex effects on a community of its internal scandals, revelations, disruptions, disappointments, and catastrophes. Any associate professor who is paying attention will have heard comedies and tragedies that make even a Coleman Silk seem ordinary. I find this simplification of academic psychology most glaring in the sagas of sexual harassment that have dominated in recent years.

Let me take as an example one I haven't yet discussed in these pages, *Nemesis* (1990), written by Joyce Carol Oates under her pseudonym (usually employed for genre fiction), Rosamond Smith. Although I am not exactly a character in this novel, it was partly based on, or inspired by, a notorious case of sexual harassment in the English department at Princeton. In the earlier chapters, describing the opening-year party given by the director of graduate studies,

Maggie Blackburn, for the faculty and students of the music department, after which a famous professor named Rolfe Christensen as-
saults a young male graduate student named Brendan Bauer, Oates
deals in depth with the effects of this scandal on the community and
the response of the university. As a Princeton faculty member, and
longtime sharp-eyed observer of the frailties of the academic milieu,
she is among the best and most tough-minded fictional analysts of
university trauma. Invariably she grasps its swings between horror
and farce, its networks of malicious gossip, its combinations of political ambition and intellectual idealism. Oates/Smith writes brilliantly
about Maggie's shock when the campus rumor mill begins to turn on
her: "In some quarters—misogynist rather than gay—it was believed
that Maggie Blackburn was a militant feminist who had launched a
personal vendetta against Rolfe Christensen; with the complicity of
one of her students, she had maneuvered the elder composer into
being suspended from his job."[1] Naturally, Maggie's "friends" take
care that she should hear this rumor. It's an interesting plot twist,
and in novels by Roth and Prose, the idea that feminists and others
set up entrapment schemes for male professors has become standard.
But Oates/Smith does not stay with Maggie's feelings about these
rumors, or with the threats, warnings, and hostilities that come to
surround all parties in a sexual-harassment case. Old resentments
and prejudices reemerge; the protective armor of mutual ignorance
that passes for collegiality in many departments cracks, and while
some are shocked to realize how little they knew about their old
friends and colleagues, others are appalled to learn how shallow the
affable façade of collegiality is. Harsh and puritanical judgments
from some quarters, silent guilt and self-questioning in others—for
few professors can survive an academic career without acknowledging the erotic tensions of teaching—pervade in an atmosphere thick
with emotion.

  Not even Oates/Smith can fully capture the emotional fallout and
the complex sense of absurdity, injustice, foolishness, sorrow, anger,
and disillusion that comes with the territory of sexual harassment
and other academic scandals. Perhaps I am leaning too hard on this
one book—we all know that when we have been personally involved
in an event, we are more critical readers of descriptions of it, whether
they are in the *New York Times* or in a novel. *Nemesis* also differs

from the standard academic-sexual-harassment novel in taking on a case of homosexual assault—a much more fraught and unconventional plot than the heterosexual one. The raw material of this case strikes so deeply at core ideas about masculinity and the unspoken contracts of academic society that it would have even challenged Oates writing under her own name in a full-length serious literary novel to encompass it. Nonetheless, I feel sure that overall, the topic of sexual harassment has reverberations beyond its treatment by even our best contemporary writers. The great American novel about this particular campus trauma has yet to be written.

In another sense, academic novels are too sensational and apocalyptic. Usually—or simultaneously—professors are more concerned with whether the book we need will be in the library than with disciplinary hearings or extramarital affairs or murder plots. But overall the daily life of a professor is not good narrative material. I haven't found any novel that really captures the intensity of academic time, its peculiar mix of the quotidian and minute task with the daunting awareness of eternity. There can be a hint of academic careerism in any catastrophe; rendering that combination of calculation and grief is a lot for novelists to take on.

I suspect that what's needed in academic fiction is a more historicized view, a viewpoint that accepts the decline in the ideals of the academy while acknowledging the inevitability of such transformations within institutions. Those who live permanently in the institutions—the faculty—will feel these changes the most. It's been said that in every marriage there are really two marriages—that of the wife and that of the husband. (Freud would add the marriages of the in-laws). In the university, I think there are two stories—those of the faculty and those of the students. Despite high expenses, cutbacks, issues of affirmative action, complaints about standards, from a student perspective, academic life is flourishing. More young people than ever before in history want and expect to go to college. Their undergraduate experience continues to bring satisfaction, pleasure, and happiness. Today's undergraduates have better research facilities, educational opportunities, counseling, living arrangements, scholarship aid, food, and social options than ever before. At most campuses they are happy; at some, deliriously so.

But I can't say the same about the faculty. College and university teaching is good work, nice work, as David Lodge says. But it's not utopia. In his splendid academic novel *Home* (2001), Hazard Adams uses a real American utopian community, "Home," as a metaphor for the contemporary English department as a failed utopia. Adams is wonderfully placed to pronounce on these matters. A distinguished critic and literary theorist who is Professor Emeritus of Comparative Literature at the University of Washington, he has written two other academic novels, *The Horses of Instruction*, set in the 1950s, and *Many Pretty Toys*, set in 1970–71.

In *Home*, history professor and ex-administrator Edward Williams is studying the nineteenth-century anarchist community called "Home" and chairing the external review committee of the English department at State. He can't help seeing parallels between the two: "He had begun to think that with some severe qualifications an anarchist model—but not communal, Home style—might fit to describe" the English department, where professors who had "pretty much forgotten its long colorful history of dispute with the administration, the legislature, and maybe the world or the real now fought among themselves for power."[2] The department is fighting about an appointment to the Morgan Professorship of America Literature and Culture, which it has been trying and failing to make for three years. "The reasons had been various, but . . . the disagreements had become political in the way that the whole profession had seemed to become politicized. Race, class, gender, the canon of great works, Western culture, multiculturalism, diversity—all these words buzzed around the simplest question of curriculum or faculty recruitment." But the buzz conceals a much deeper problem that the department does not want to confront—its own survival. "The real threat was elsewhere and from without: what the university, increasingly co-opted by technologically oriented businesses, would do (if anything) with or to the humanities. Would one day someone visit an English department as he was visiting Home only to find it gone?" (7).

These questions of the decline and fall of English departments in the twenty-first century are very serious, not just because business, science, and technology have so much power, but because the departments have lost their sense of purpose and do not have the will to find a new intellectual center. "Centers," Williams reflects, " . . . had been out of fashion for years" (9). His views are seconded by Helen Grant, a scholar of seventeenth-century prose and a former English department chair who has been long serving as dean of the faculty at State. Listening to the complaints of various professors coming to campaign for the new appointment, Grant has to "remind herself that the Morgan Professorship was important to many people. She'd well learned that literature wasn't the center of any universe known to universities, if it had ever been" (21).

But the members of the department act as if they *were* the center of the universe. They continue to squabble about the appointment and ignore much deeper issues about the future as they drift into obsolescence, with less self-awareness than the members of the utopian community when faced with their own destruction by outside forces. Inevitably, because it has now become the template for expressing all conflict, there is a sexual-harassment case in the English department at State. A feminist professor, Francine Wright, encourages an undergraduate to complain to the dean that she has been harassed by a male professor, Harley Wales, at a department party. (Wright and Wales are on different sides about the appointment.) In fact, Wales is secretly gay. In conversation with Dean Grant, the student confesses that she is unsure any incident took place, withdraws her complaint, and takes a leave of absence from school. Nevertheless, the rumors continue to spread. Students demonstrate for Wales's dismissal; he files a libel suit against Wright; the two actually come to blows.

Francine is tormented by conscience: "She had allowed the self that she had become to happen. She'd killed some earlier self with malevolence, misplaced hatred. . . . Beginning with the best of intentions, with commitment to justice, to fairness, to what was right, she had somehow lost her balance and fallen into a condition of hate" (201). She kills herself. But ironically, her death makes her even more of a campus heroine and fails to exonerate Wales: "As her stock rose, Harley Wales's plummeted, for it still seemed to many that he had been her tormentor. What had appeared as comedy, even farce, some department members now classified in the genre of tragedy with Francine the heroine" (204).

Adams contrasts the pettiness, intransigence, and unkindness of the members of the English department with the courage, loyalty, compassion, and solidarity of the members of the Home commune, many of whom were persecuted and imprisoned for their belief in free speech. But in the end, Home, like the department, lost its identity through "ideological disagreements [that] had exacerbated personal idiosyncrasies into hatreds" (178). Elegiac and muted rather than condemnatory and dramatic, *Home* reflects sadly on the end of the dream that a group of people dedicated and devoted to literature, culture, scholarship, and teaching could form a utopian community of fellowship, affection, and mutual support.

Well, all utopias are boring in the end. The current bitterness of academic fiction may be exaggerated, but perhaps it is healthier and wiser not to harbor idyllic fantasies about English departments and their inhabitants. It wouldn't have been wonderful to have Edward Casaubon for a colleague either, but Eliot's portrait of a scholar, if bleak, is powerful and profound. What I hope I've learned from reading academic novels, in addition to the inside dope on the Guggie letter, is not to underestimate the activity of the quiet corridors and quadrangles of the academic world and to expect, as George Eliot said in *Middlemarch*, that if we could really understand even a fraction of what is being thought and felt within them, we would be stunned by the roar on the other side of silence.

Notes

INTRODUCTION

1. Richard G. Caram, "The Secular Priests: A Study of the College Professor as Hero in Selected American Fiction, 1955–1977" (Ph.D. diss., St. Louis University, 1980).

2. Sanford Pinsker, "Who Cares If Roger Ackroyd Gets Tenure?" *Partisan Review* 66:3 (summer 1999): 439.

3. John Updike, Foreword, *The Early Stories* (New York: Knopf, 2003), xiv.

4. Ian Carter, *Ancient Cultures of Conceit: British University Fiction in the Post-War Years* (London: Routledge, 1990), 15.

5. Jay Parini, "The Fictional Campus: Sex, Power, and Despair," *Chronicle of Higher Education* (September 22, 2000): B12.

6. Steven Connor, *The English Novel in History, 1950–1995* (London and New York: Routledge, 1995), 69–71.

7. Janice Rossen, *The University in Modern Fiction* (New York: St. Martin's Press, 1993), 3, 9.

8. Pinsker, 440.

9. Connor, 73.

10. Lee R. Edwards, "Women, Energy, and *Middlemarch*," in *Middlemarch*, ed. Bert G. Hornback (New York: Norton, 1977), 692.

11. Willa Cather, *The Professor's House* (1925; New York: Vintage, 1990), 257.

12. Hazard Adams, *The Academic Tribes*, 2nd ed. (Urbana and Chicago: University of Illinois Press, 1988), 82.

13. John Kenneth Galbraith, *A Tenured Professor* (Boston: Houghton Mifflin, 1990), 39.

14. Nancy K. Miller, *But Enough About Me* (New York: Columbia University Press, 2002), xiv.

15. Adams, 97, 99.

16. Gerald Brace Warner, *The Department* (Chicago and London: University of Chicago Press, 1983), 224–25.

17. Jay Parini, "Every September a Clean Slate and a Fresh Start," *Chronicle of Higher Education*, September 10, 1999, A80.

18. Malcolm Bradbury, *The History Man* (Boston: Houghton Mifflin, 1976), 1.

19. Bradbury, 217.

20. C. P. Snow, *The Masters* (London: House of Stratus, 2000), 3.

21. Richard Russo, *Straight Man* (New York: Random House, 1997), 8.

22. Mary McCarthy, *The Groves of Academe* (New York: Signet, 1963), 206.

CHAPTER I

1. C. P. Snow, *The Masters* (London: House of Stratus, 2000), 344, 345. Further references will be given parenthetically in the text.

2. Malcolm Bradbury, *The Modern British Novel* (London: Penguin, 1993), 320.

3. David Lodge, "Lucky Jim Revisited," in *The Practice of Writing* (London: Allen Lane, 1997), 84, 85, 91.

4. Janice Rossen, *The University in Modern Fiction* (New York: St. Martin's Press, 1993), 120; John Halperin, *C. P. Snow: An Oral Biography* (New York: Harvester Press, 1983), xii.

5. C. P. Snow, "Trollope's Percipience," *Trollope: His Life and Art* (New York: Scribner's, 1975), 111–12.

6. Charles Raven, *The Spectator*, March 30, 1962; quoted in Stefan Collini, introduction to C. P. Snow, *The Two Cultures* (Cambridge: Cambridge University Press, 1998), xxxviii.

7. Mark Pattison, *Memoirs*, 289–90, quoted in A. D. Nuttall, *Dead from the Waist Down: Scholars and Scholarship in Literature and the Popular Imagination* (New Haven, Conn.: Yale University Press, 2003), 81.

8. Kingsley Amis, "An Undergraduate," letter to *Time & Tide*, August 23, 1947, 138.

9. Kingsley Amis, *Lucky Jim* (New York: Viking, 1969), 26. Further references will be given parenthetically in the text.

10. Rossen, 188.

11. Malcolm Bradbury, *Who Do You Think You Are?* (London: Picador, 1976), 177.

12. Kingsley Amis, *Memoirs* (London: Hutchinson, 1991), 56.

13. Humphrey Carpenter, "The Angry Young Lesbian Fanciers," *London Times*, April 16, 2000, 10.

14. Philip Larkin, *Trouble at Willow Gables and Other Fictions*, ed. James Booth (London: Faber 2003), 423, 426.

15. Carol Brightman, *Writing Dangerously* (New York: Harcourt Brace, 1992), 431.

16. Mary McCarthy, "The Art of Fiction," *Paris Review* (Winter/Spring 1962):21–22.

17. Pinsker, "Who Cares If Roger Ackroyd Gets Tenure?" *Partisan Review* 66:3 (summer 1999): 444.

18. William Pritchard, *Randall Jarrell: A Literary Life* (New York: Farrar Strauss, 1990), 233, 235, 237.

19. Edward W. Said, *Out of Place* (New York: Vintage, 2000), 274–79.

20. Carlos Baker, *A Friend in Power* (New York: Scribner's, 1958), 170. Further references will be given parenthetically in the text.

CHAPTER 2

1. John W. Aldridge, *The Party at Cranton* (New York: David McKay, 1960), 42–43. Further references will be given parenthetically in the text.

2. Ann Waldron, "The Fictive Princeton," *Princeton Alumni Magazine*, November 4, 1998, 16.

3. Judy Newman, *Alison Lurie: A Critical Study* (Amsterdam/Atlanta, Ga.: Rodopi, 2000), 4.

4. Alison Lurie, *Familiar Spirits* (New York: Viking, 2001), 15, 21–22.

5. Alison Lurie, *Love and Friendship* (New York: Avon, 1970), 20.

6. Carolyn Heilbrun, *Writing a Woman's Life* (New York: Ballantine 1988), 51–52.

7. Amanda Cross, *The James Joyce Murder* (New York: Ballantine, 1982), 132–33.

8. Bernard Malamud, "Reflections of a Writer: Long Work, Short Life," *New York Times Book Review*, March 20, 1988, 15. Accessed April 27, 2004, at http://www.nytimes.com/books/97/09/28/reviews/malamud-reflections.html.

9. Philip Roth, "Pictures of Malamud," *New York Times*, April 20, 1986; section 7, p. 1.

10. Malcolm Bradbury, *Dangerous Pilgrimages* (London: Secker and Warburg, 1995), 455, 456.

11. Malcolm Bradbury, *Stepping Westward* (London: Arena, 1989), 9. Further references will be given parenthetically in the text.

12. Charles Brady, *Buffalo Evening News*, September 21, 1968, p. B-12.

13. Gerald Warner Brace, *The Department*, original ed. (New York: Norton, 1968); citations from Phoenix ed. (Chicago: University of Chicago Press, 1983), 13, 266. Further references will be given parenthetically in the text.

14. Henry Nash Smith, "Something Is Happening But You Don't Know What It Is, Do You Mr. Jones?" in *PMLA Millennium Issue* 115 (December 2000): 1905.

CHAPTER 3

1. Malcolm Bradbury, *The History Man* (Boston: Houghton Mifflin, 1976), 58, 3, 62. Further references will be given parenthetically in the text. Neither the OED nor Google has anything to say on "eolipilic," but that's what the book says.

2. Tom Driver, quoted in Susan Kress, *Carolyn G. Heilbrun: Feminist in a Tenured Position* (Charlottesville: University Press of Virginia, 1997), 82.

3. Amanda Cross, *Poetic Justice* (New York: Avon, 1979), 11. Further references will be given parenthetically in the text.

4. Robert Bernard, *Deadly Meeting* (New York: W. W. Norton, 1970). Robert B. Martin died in 1999.

5. Joyce Carol Oates, "Angst," *The Hungry Ghosts* (Los Angeles: Black Sparrow, 1974), 195. Further references will be given parenthetically in the text. In December 1971, Oates participated in an MLA session on her work in Chicago, chaired by Sister Edna Eileen Byrne of Our Lady of Holy Cross College.

6. Joyce Carol Oates, letter in *New York Times Book Review*, September 22, 1974, 43.

7. Gail Godwin, *The Odd Woman* (New York: Knopf, 1974), 207. Further references will be given parenthetically in the text.

8. Nicci Gerrard, Introduction, *The Odd Woman* (London: Virago, 2000), vii, viii.

9. Rachel Brownstein, "The Odd Woman and Literary Feminism," in *American Women Writing Fiction*, ed. Mickey Pearlman (Lexington: University Press of Kentucky, 1989), 173–84.

10. Gerrard, ix.

11. Bradbury, 65. Further references will be given parenthetically in the text.

12. *The Sunday Times*, 1981, quoted in John Haffenden, *Novelists in Interview* (London: Methuen, 1985), 26.

13. Haffenden, 41.

14. David Lodge, "He Was My Literary Twin," *The Guardian*, November 29, 2000.

15. David Lodge, "Fact and Fiction in the Novel," *The Practice of Writing* (London: Penguin, 1997), 32–33.

16. David Lodge, interview with John Haffenden, *Novelists in Interview* (London: Methuen, 1985), 161.

17. David Lodge, *Changing Places: A Tale of Two Campuses* (London: Secker and Warburg, 1975), 3. Further references will be given parenthetically in the text.

18. Haffenden, 164.

19. Larissa MacFarquhar, "The Dean's List: The Enfant Terrible of English Lit Grows Up," *The New Yorker*, June 11, 2001, pp. 65–66, 71.

20. Philip Roth, *The Professor of Desire* (1977), Vintage International Ed. (New York: Vintage/Random House, 1984).

21. Philip Roth, *The Ghost Writer* (1979), Vintage International Ed. (New York: Vintage/Random House, 1995).

22. Philip Roth, *Reading Myself and Others*, Vintage International Ed. (New York: Vintage/Random House, 2001), 144.

CHAPTER 4

1. Amanda Cross, *Death in a Tenured Position* (New York: Ballantine, 1988), 5, 9. Further references will be given parenthetically in the text.

2. Carolyn G. Heilbrun, *The Last Gift of Time: Life Beyond Sixty* (New York; Ballantine, 1997), 120–21.

3. Carolyn G. Heilbrun, "Bringing the Spirit Back to English Studies," reprinted in *The Feminist Critical Revolution*, ed. Elaine Showalter (New York: Pantheon, 1985), 21–28.

4. Joyce Carol Oates, *Marya: A Life* (New York: Dutton, 1986). Page references will be given parenthetically in the text.

5. Alison Lurie, *Foreign Affairs* (New York: Random House, 1984), 18. Further references will be given parenthetically in the text.

6. Rebecca Goldstein, *The Mind-Body Problem*, 1983 (New York: Penguin, 1993), 12–13.

7. Joan Smith, *A Masculine Ending* (New York: Fawcett Crest, 1987).

8. Don DeLillo, *White Noise* (New York: Penguin, 1986). Page references will be given parenthetically in the text.

9. Interview with Ray Suarez, August 4, 1994, on NPR Book Club of the Air. Quoted from the transcription at http://perival.com/delillo/technoise.html, accessed April 25, 2004.

10. David R. Shumway, "The Star System in Literary Studies," *PMLA* (1997): 90, 91.

11. Elaine Showalter, "Interview with David Lodge," *Profession* (1999): 10.

12. Stanley Fish, interview, "Thinking in the 20th Century," (1985), quoted in Shumway, 85.

13. Serge Doubrovsky, *Un amour de soi* (Paris: Hachette, 1982), 271–72. Translation by English Showalter.

14. David Lodge, interview in John Haffenden, *Novelists in Interview* (London: Methuen, 1985), 65.

15. David Lodge, "Prologue," *Small World* (London: Secker and Warburg, 1984). Further references will be given parenthetically in the text.

16. Carol Shields, *Swann* (New York/London: Penguin, 1987), 148. Further references will be given parenthetically in the text.

17. David Lodge, *Nice Work* (New York: Viking, 1988). Page references will be given parenthetically in the text.

18. Elizabeth Gaskell, *North and South*, ed. Dorothy Collin and Martin Dodsworth (Harmondsworth: Penguin Books, 1970), 66–68.

CHAPTER 5

1. Blair French, *The Ticking Tenure Clock* (Albany, N.Y.: SUNY Press, 1998), 3.

2. Stephanie Merritt, *Gaveston* (London: Faber and Faber, 2002), 25.

3. Shannon Olson, *Welcome to My Planet*, 2000 (New York: Penguin, 2001), 89.

4. Hazard Adams, *The Academic Tribes* (Urbana and Chicago: University of Illinois Press, 1988), 90.

5. Gordon Hutner, "What We Talk about When We Talk about Hiring," *Profession* (1994): 76.

6. D. J. H. Jones, *Murder at the MLA* (Athens and London: University of Georgia Press, 1993), 41. Further references will be given parenthetically in the text.

7. Percival Everett's *Erasure* (New York: Hyperion, 2001) is another, with a similar plot but in reverse. The protagonist, Thelonious "Monk" Ellison, is so disgusted by the success of a novel purporting to describe an authentic ghetto experience that he writes an outrageous travesty of the genre called *My Pafology*, a book "on which I knew I could never put my name" (62), so he signs it "Stagg R. Leigh." Random House offers a six hundred thousand dollar advance, and the book becomes a huge success, as does a later effort titled *Fuck*, which receives a major award as the novel ends. Either way, the black intellectual is trapped in an inauthentic role.

8. Ishmael Reed, *Japanese by Spring* (New York: Athenaeum, 1993), 6.

9. John L'Heureux, *The Handmaid of Desire* (New York: Soho Press, 1996). Further references will be given parenthetically in the text.

10. James Hynes, *Publish and Perish: Three Tales of Tenure and Terror* (New York: Picador, 1997), 21. Further references will be given parenthetically in the text.

11. A. S. Byatt, *Possession: A Romance* (New York: Random House, 1990), 12. Further references will be given parenthetically in the text.

12. Catherine Burgass, *A. S. Byatt's Possession* (London/New York: Continuum Contemporaries, 2002), 34.

13. Joanne Dobson, *Quieter Than Sleep*, 1997 (New York: Bantam, 1998).

14. Joanne Dobson, *The Northbury Papers*, 1998 (New York: Bantam, 1999), 6.

15. Dobson, *Northbury Papers*, 60.

16. Dobson, *Quieter Than Sleep*, 3, 215, 154.

17. Joanne Dobson, *The Raven and the Nightingale*, 1999 (New York: Bantam, 2000), 13.

18. Richard Russo, *Straight Man* (London: Vintage, 1998), xii. Further references will be given parenthetically in the text.

19. Lev Raphael, *The Death of a Constant Lover* (New York: Walker, 1999), 5. Further references will be given parenthetically in the text.

20. J. M. Coetzee, *Disgrace* (New York: Viking, 1999), 3. Further references will be given parenthetically in the text.

21. "David Mamet Meets Alan Dershowitz," conversation reported in 1995 by Richard Stayton, accessed April 26, 2004, at http://home.comcast.net/~jasoncharnick/mamet.html. Dershowitz claims, "It's like a witchhunt here at Harvard," and adds, "I'm writing a novel about date rape."

CHAPTER 6

1. Sarah Boxer, "Satire in the Ivory Tower Gets Rough," *New York Times*, October 21, 2000, B9.

2. Francine Prose, *Blue Angel* (New York: HarperCollins, 2000), 8. Further page references will be given parenthetically in the text.

3. Philip Roth, *The Human Stain*, 2000 (New York: Vintage, 2001), 6–7. Further references will be given parenthetically in the text.

4. James Lasdun, *The Horned Man* (London: Vintage, 2002), 16, 17. Further references will be given parenthetically in the text.

5. James Hynes, *The Lecturer's Tale* (New York: Picador USA, 2001). Page references will be given parenthetically in the text.

6. Tobin Harshaw, "Wanton Deconstruction," review of James Hynes, *The Lecturer's Tale, New York Times Book Review*, January 21, 2001, p. 30.

7. Jonathan Franzen, *The Corrections* (New York: Farrar, Straus and Giroux, 2001), 33–34. Further references will be given parenthetically in the text.

8. Saul Bellow, *Ravelstein*, 2000 (New York: Penguin, 2001). Page references will be given parenthetically in the text.

CONCLUSION

1. Rosamund Smith, *Nemesis* (New York: Dutton, 1990), 79.

2. Hazard Adams, *Home* (Albany: SUNY Press, 2001), 2. Further references will be given parenthetically in the text.

Bibliography of
Academic Novels

Adams, Hazard. *Home.* Albany: SUNY Press, 2001.

Aldridge, John W. *The Party at Cranton.* New York: David McKay, 1960.

Amis, Kingsley. *Lucky Jim* (1953). New York: Viking, 1969.

Baker, Carlos. *A Friend in Power.* New York: Scribner's, 1958.

Bellow, Saul. *Ravelstein* (2000). New York: Penguin, 2001.

Bernard, Robert (pseudonym of Robert B. Martin). *Deadly Meeting.* New York: W. W. Norton, 1970.

Brace, Gerald Warner. *The Department* (1968). Chicago and London: University of Chicago Press, 1988.

Bradbury, Malcolm. *Dangerous Pilgrimages.* London: Secker and Warburg, 1995.

———. *The History Man* (1975). Boston: Houghton Mifflin, 1976.

———. *Stepping Westward* (1965). London: Arena, 1989.

———. *Who Do You Think You Are?* London: Picador, 1976.

Byatt, A. S. *Possession.* New York: Random House, 1990.

Cather, Willa. *The Professor's House* (1925). New York: Vintage, 1990.

Coetzee, J. M. *Disgrace.* New York: Viking, 1999.

Cross, Amanda (pseudonym of Carolyn Heilbrun). *Death in a Tenured Position* (1981). New York: Ballantine, 1988.

———. *In the Last Analysis* (1964). New York: Ballantine, 1992.

———. *The James Joyce Murder* (1976). New York: Ballantine, 1982.

———. *Poetic Justice* (1970). New York: Avon, 1979.

DeLillo, Don. *White Noise* (1985). New York: Penguin, 1986.

Dobson, Joanne. *The Northbury Papers* (1998). New York: Bantam, 1999.

———. *Quieter Than Sleep* (1997). New York: Bantam, 1998.

———. *The Raven and the Nightingale* (1999). New York: Bantam, 2000.

Doubrovsky, Serge. *Un amour de soi.* Paris: Hachette, 1982.

Eliot, George. *Middlemarch* (1871–72). Norton Critical Ed. by Bert G. Hornback. New York: Norton, 1977.

Everett, Percival. *Erasure*. New York: Hyperion, 2001.

French, Blair. *The Ticking Tenure Clock*. Albany: SUNY Press, 1998.

Galbraith, John Kenneth. *A Tenured Professor*. Boston: Houghton Mifflin, 1990.

Gaskell, Elizabeth. *North and South* (1854–55). Ed. Dorothy Collin and Martin Dodsworth. Harmondsworth: Penguin Books, 1970.

Godwin, Gail. *The Odd Woman*. New York: Knopf, 1974.

Goldstein, Rebecca. *The Mind-Body Problem* (1983). New York: Penguin, 1993.

Hynes, James. *The Lecturer's Tale*. New York: Picador USA, 2001.

———. *Publish and Perish: Three Tales of Tenure and Terror*. New York: Picador, 1997.

Jones, D. J. H. *Murder at the MLA*. Athens and London: University of Georgia Press, 1993.

Larkin, Philip. *Trouble at Willow Gables and Other Fictions*. Ed. James Booth. London: Faber 2003.

Lasdun, James. *The Horned Man*. London: Vintage, 2002.

L'Heureux, John. *The Handmaid of Desire*. New York: Soho Press, 1996.

Lodge, David. *Changing Places: A Tale of Two Campuses*. London: Secker and Warburg, 1975.

———. *Nice Work*. New York: Viking, 1988.

———. "Prologue," *Small World*. London: Secker and Warburg, 1984.

Lurie, Alison. *Familiar Spirits*. New York: Viking, 2001.

———. *Foreign Affairs*. New York: Random House, 1984.

———. *Love and Friendship* (1962). New York: Avon, 1970.

———. *The War between the Tates* (1974). New York: Random House, 1974.

Malamud, Bernard. *A New Life*. New York: Farrar Straus Cudahy, 1961.

McCarthy, Mary. *The Groves of Academe* (1951). New York: Signet, 1963.

Merritt, Stephanie. *Gaveston*. London: Faber and Faber, 2002.

Oates, Joyce Carol. "Angst," *The Hungry Ghosts*. Los Angeles: Black Sparrow 1974.

———. *Marya: A Life*. New York: Dutton, 1986.

Olson, Shannon. *Welcome to My Planet*. New York: Penguin, 2000.

Prose, Francine. *Blue Angel*. New York: HarperCollins, 2000.

Raphael, Lev. *The Death of a Constant Lover*. New York: Walker, 1999.

Reed, Ishmael. *Japanese by Spring*. New York: Athenaeum, 1993.

Roth, Philip. *The Ghost Writer* (1979). Vintage International Ed. New York: Vintage/Random House, 1995.

———. *The Human Stain* (2000). New York: Vintage, 2001.

———. *The Professor of Desire* (1977). Vintage International Ed. New York: Vintage/Random House, 1984.

Russo, Richard. *Straight Man*. New York: Random House, 1997.

Sayers, Dorothy L. *Gaudy Night* (1936). New York: Avon, 1968.

Shields, Carol. *Swann* (1987). New York: Penguin, 1990.

————. *Unless*. London: Fourth Estate, 2001.

Smith, Joan. *A Masculine Ending*. New York: Fawcett Crest, 1987.

Smith, Rosamund (pseudonym of Joyce Carol Oates). *Nemesis*. New York: Dutton, 1990.

Snow, C. P. *The Masters* (1951). London: House of Stratus, 2000.

Tartt, Donna. *The Secret History*. New York: Knopf, 1992.

Trollope, Anthony. *Barchester Towers* (1857). New York: Penguin, 1983.

Index

Adams, Hazard, 8, 9, 88; *Home,* 122–24

Adams, Henry, 31

Aldridge, John W., *The Party at Cranton,* 35–38, 57, 118

Alfred, William, 71

Amis, Kingsley, *Lucky Jim,* 14–15, 23–26, 33, 118

Un amour de soi (Doubrovsky), 79–80

"Angst" (Oates), 54–55

Arendt, Hannah, *Origins of Totalitarianism,* 30

Aristophanes, *The Clouds,* 2

Arnold, Matthew, 57

Auden, W. H., 50

Austen, Jane, 39

Baker, Carlos, 36; *A Friend in Power,* 30–33, 57

Barchester Towers (Trollope), 5

Bate, Walter Jackson, 71

Bellow, Saul, 100; *Ravelstein,* 115–17

Bernard, Robert. *See* Martin, Robert B.

Bishop, Jonathan, 38

Blackmur, Richard, 35, 36, 38

Bloom, Alan, 116; *The Closing of the American Mind,* 115

Blue Angel (Prose), 101–3, 104, 106

Boxer, Sarah, 100

Brace, Gerald Warner, *The Department,* 9–10, 46–48

Bradbury, Malcolm: "An Extravagant Fondness for the Love of Women," 24; *The History Man,* 3, 7, 10–11, 49–50, 58–61, 100; *The Modern British Novel,* 15; *Stepping Westward,* 42, 44–45

Brownstein, Rachel, 56

Butler, Rab, 22

Byatt, A. S., *Possession,* 7, 11, 91–94, 96

Byrne, Sister Edna Eileen, 128n.5

Carter, Ian, 3

Cather, Willa, *The Professor's House,* 6

Changing Places (Lodge), 62–66, 67

Chaucer, Geoffrey, *The Canterbury Tales,* 110

Clinton, Bill, 104, 107

The Closing of the American Mind
  (Bloom), 115
The Clouds (Aristophanes), 2
Coburn, Kathleen, 92
Coetzee, J. M., *Disgrace,* 98–99,
  100–101, 103, 104, 106
Connor, Steven, 3, 4
The Corrections (Franzen), 111–15
Cross, Amanda. *See* Heilbrun,
  Carolyn

David Copperfield (Dickens), 110
Deadly Meeting (Bernard/Martin),
  52–54
Death in a Tenured Position
  (Cross/Heilbrun), 68–73
Death of a Constant Lover
  (Raphael), 97–98
DeLillo, Don, *White Noise,* 76–78,
  111
The Department (Brace), 9–10,
  46–48
Dershowitz, Alan, 131n.21
Dickens, Charles, *David
  Copperfield,* 110
Disgrace (Coetzee), 98–99, 100–101,
  103, 104, 106
Dobson, Joanne, 7; *The Northbury
  Papers,* 94, 95–96; *Quieter Than
  Sleep,* 94–95; *The Raven and the
  Nightingale,* 94, 96
Doubrovsky, Serge, *Un amour de
  soi,* 79–80
Driver, Tom, 50

Eliot, George, *Middlemarch,* 5–6, 7,
  39, 40, 124
Everett, Percival, *Erasure,* 130n.7
"An Extravagant Fondness for
  the Love of Women" (Bradbury),
  24

Fetterley, Judith, 94
Fish, Stanley, 5, 64–66, 79, 85;
  Surprised by Sin, 109
Foreign Affairs (Lurie), 41, 74–75
Franzen, Jonathan, *The Corrections,*
  111–15
French, Blair, *The Ticking Tenure
  Clock,* 87
A Friend in Power (Baker), 30–33,
  57
Frye, Northrop, 9

Galbraith, John Kenneth, 8
Gaskell, Elizabeth, *North and South,*
  7, 83
Gaudy Night (Sayers), 6–7
Gaveston (Merritt), 87
Gerrard, Nicci, 55–56, 58
The Ghost Writer (Roth), 66, 67
Gilbert, Sandra, *Masterpiece Theater,* 5
Gissing, George, *The Odd Women,*
  7, 56–57
Godwin, Gail, *The Odd Woman,* 7,
  55–58, 84
Goldstein, Rebecca, *The Mind-Body
  Problem,* 75
The Groves of Academe (McCarthy),
  27–30, 33, 118
Gubar, Susan, *Masterpiece Theater,* 5

Halperin, John, 15
The Handmaid of Desire
  (L'Heureux), 90–91
Heilbrun, Carolyn (*pseud.* Amanda
  Cross), 41–42; *Death in a
  Tenured Position,* 68–73; *In the
  Last Analysis,* 42; *The James Joyce
  Murder,* 42; *Poetic Justice,* 50–52
Hillyer, Robert, 38
The History Man (Bradbury), 3, 7,
  10–11, 49–50, 58–61, 100

Home (H. Adams), 122–24
The Horned Man (Lasdun), 107–8,
    111
The Human Stain (Roth), 103–7
Hynes, James: *The Lecturer's Tale*, 2,
    108–11; *Publish and Perish*, 7, 91

In the Last Analysis
    (Cross/Heilbrun), 42
Ishiguro, Kazuo, *The Remains of the
    Day*, 48

Jackson, David, 38
The James Joyce Murder
    (Cross/Heilbrun), 42
Japanese by Spring (Reed), 89–90
Jarrell, Randall, *Pictures from an
    Institution*, 30
Jones, D. J. H., *Murder at the MLA*,
    88–89
Joyce, James, 42

Kaakinen, Jop, 49–50
Kirk, Grayson, 50
Kitson-Clark, George, 21–22
Kristeva, Julia, *The Samurai*, 106

Larkin, Philip, 24; "A New World
    Symphony," 26–27
Lasdun, James, *The Horned Man*,
    107–8, 111
The Last Chronicle of Barset
    (Trollope), 46
The Lecturer's Tale (Hynes), 2,
    108–11
Leigh, Ralph, 22
Lewalski, Barbara, 71
Lewis, C. S., 24
L'Heureux, John, *The Handmaid of
    Desire*, 90–91
Lodge, David, 5, 15, 61, 121–22;

Changing Places, 62–66, 67; *Nice
    Work*, 7, 82–86, 93; *Small World*,
    78–81, 88, 91–92
Love and Friendship (Lurie), 38–41
Lucky Jim (Amis), 14–15, 23–26, 33,
    118
Lurie, Alison, 9; *Foreign Affairs*, 41,
    74–75; *Love and Friendship*,
    38–41; *The War between the Tates*,
    38, 60

MacCaffrey, Isabel, 71
MacFarquhar, Larissa, 65–66
Malamud, Bernard, *A New Life*,
    42–44, 107
Mamet, David, *Oleanna*, 98, 99,
    100
Martin, Robert B. (*pseud.* Robert
    Bernard), *Deadly Meeting*, 52–54
Marya: A Life (Oates), 73
A Masculine Ending (J. Smith),
    75–76
Masterpiece Theater (Gilbert and
    Gubar), 5
The Masters (Snow): vs. Amis's
    Lucky Jim, 23–24; Cambridge life
    captured by, 21–23; characters,
    16–19; Gay as crossover academic,
    19–20; as idyllic/utopian, 14,
    22–23, 33, 98; Jago's
    ambitions/defeat, 16–18, 20–21;
    plot, 15; reception of, 15; setting,
    15; university politics in, 16–20,
    118; winter in, 11
McCarthy, Mary, 12; *The Groves of
    Academe*, 27–30, 33, 118
Merrill, James, 38
Merritt, Stephanie, *Gaveston*, 87
Middlemarch (Eliot), 5–6, 7, 39, 40,
    124
Miller, Nancy, 8, 72

Milton, John, *Paradise Lost,* 110
The Mind-Body Problem
    (Goldstein), 75
The Modern British Novel
    (Bradbury), 15
Murder at the MLA (Jones), 88–89

Nemesis (Smith/Oates), 119–21
A New Life (Malamud), 42–44, 107
"A New World Symphony"
    (Larkin), 26–27
Nice Work (Lodge), 7, 82–86, 93
1984 (Orwell), 110
North and South (Gaskell), 7, 83
The Northbury Papers (Dobson), 94,
    95–96

Oates, Joyce Carol (*pseud.*
    Rosamond Smith), 128n.5;
    "Angst," 54–55; *Marya: A Life,*
    73; *Nemesis,* 119–21
The Odd Woman (Godwin), 7,
    55–58, 84
The Odd Women (Gissing), 7, 56–57
Oleanna (Mamet), 98, 99, 100
Olson, Shannon, *Welcome to My*
    Planet, 87–88
Origins of Totalitarianism (Arendt),
    30
Orlando (Woolf), 109
Orwell, George, *1984,* 110
Out of Place (Said), 30

Paradise Lost (Milton), 110
Parini, Jay, 3, 10
The Party at Cranton (Aldridge),
    35–38, 57, 118
Pattison, Mark, 22
Pictures from an Institution (Jarrell),
    30
Pinsker, Sanford, 2, 4, 29

Poetic Justice (Cross/Heilbrun),
    50–52
Possession (Byatt), 7, 11, 91–94, 96
The Professor of Desire (Roth),
    66–67
The Professor's House (Cather), 6
Prose, Francine, 100, 120; *Blue*
    Angel, 101–3, 104, 106
Publish and Perish (Hynes), 7, 91

Quieter Than Sleep (Dobson), 94–95

Raphael, Lev, *Death of a Constant*
    Lover, 97–98
Ravelstein (Bellow), 115–17
Raven, Charles, 21
The Raven and the Nightingale
    (Dobson), 94, 96
Reed, Ishmael, *Japanese by Spring,*
    89–90
The Remains of the Day (Ishiguro),
    48
Rossen, Janice, 3–4, 15
Roth, Philip, 43, 100, 116, 120; *The*
    Ghost Writer, 66, 67; *The Human*
    Stain, 103–7; *The Professor of*
    Desire, 66–67
Rudd, Mark, 50
Russo, Richard, 12; *Straight Man,*
    96–97

Sackville-West, Vita, 109
Said, Edward, 36; *Out of Place,* 30
The Samurai (Kristeva), 106
Sayers, Dorothy L., 41–42; *Gaudy*
    Night, 6–7
The Secret History (Tartt), 11
Sedgwick, Eve, 20
Shakespeare, William, *The Tempest,*
    110
Shields, Carol, 9; *Swann,* 81–82, 92

Shumway, David R., 78–79

Small World (Lodge), 78–81, 88, 91–92

Smith, Henry Nash, 47–48

Smith, Joan, *A Masculine Ending,* 75–76

Smith, Rosamond. *See* Oates, Joyce Carol

Snow, C. P., 5, 46, 85. See also *The Masters*

Stepping Westward (Bradbury), 42, 44–45

Straight Man (Russo), 96–97

Surprised by Sin (Fish), 109

Swann (Shields), 81–82, 92

Tartt, Donna, *The Secret History,* 11

Taylor, Laurie, 5

The Tempest (Shakespeare), 110

The Ticking Tenure Clock (French), 87

Tolkien, J. R. R., 24

Trilling, Lionel, 51

Trollope, Anthony, 16; *Barchester Towers,* 5; *The Last Chronicle of Barset,* 46

Updike, John, 2

Vendler, Helen, 71

Waldron, Ann, 36

The War between the Tates (Lurie), 38, 60

Waters, Lindsay, 66

Welcome to My Planet (Olson), 87–88

White Noise (DeLillo), 76–78, 111

Woolf, Virginia, 21; *Orlando,* 109

Acknowledgments

The Council for Research in the Humanities at Princeton sponsored my research for this book, and two wonderful student research assistants, Eben Harrell and Adena Spingarn, helped me track down novels. My Princeton colleague Michael Goldman suggested the title. At the University of Pennsylvania Press, Jerry Singerman was encouraging, patient, and resourceful. Many thanks to him, and to the Press's excellent staff of editors. Most of all, my husband, English Showalter, longtime partner in my ivory tower for two, contributed to the ideas, choices, and words.